NAVIGATING THE LEAP INTO PRIVATE PRACTICE

The Ultimate Guide to Transforming Clinical Skills into a Thriving, Purpose-driven Career

JODIE SHERATON

First published by Ultimate World Publishing 2025
Copyright © 2025 Jodie Sheraton

ISBN

Paperback: 978-1-923583-22-1
Ebook: 978-1-923583-23-8

Jodie Sheraton has asserted her rights under the Copyright, Designs and Patents Act 1988 to be identified as the author of this work. The information in this book is based on the author's experiences and opinions. The publisher specifically disclaims responsibility for any adverse consequences which may result from use of the information contained herein. Permission to use information has been sought by the author. Any breaches will be rectified in further editions of the book.

All rights reserved. No part of this publication may be reproduced, stored in or introduced into a retrieval system, or transmitted in any form, or by any means (electronic, mechanical, photocopying, recording or otherwise) without the prior written permission of the author. Any person who does any unauthorised act in relation to this publication may be liable to criminal prosecution and civil claims for damages. Enquiries should be made through the publisher.

Cover design: Ultimate World Publishing
Layout and typesetting: Ultimate World Publishing
Editor: Maddie Johnson

Ultimate World Publishing
Diamond Creek,
Victoria Australia 3089
www.writeabook.com.au

Testimonials

"While dietitians are highly trained in clinical care, navigating the realities of business requires a different skill set. Jodie has created a clear and practical guide that bridges this gap, combining clinical expertise with business know-how. The Confident Dietitian is an inspiring resource that empowers dietitians at every stage of their private practice journey to step forward with confidence, clarity, and purpose. This is a must-read for every dietitian ready to build a thriving, sustainable, values-driven career in private practice."

Maree Ferguson, CEO & Founder, Dietitian Connection

"This book is the must-have guide for new graduate dietitians embarking on a career in private practice or those seeking to expand and grow their businesses. Jodie shares her wealth of wisdom, experience, and expertise with generosity, offering support and inspiration in an empowering way. Blending both motivation and practical know-how, the book provides a clear roadmap to building a profitable and sustainable practice. Beyond the fundamentals, Jodie imparts invaluable real-world lessons equipping practitioners with actionable guidance, fresh perspectives, and intelligent business tools to design a purposeful and fulfilling career."

Jennifer Donnelly, APD

"This book will take your private practice journey to the next level. Whether you're new to the field, part of a team, or an experienced business owner, Jodie's practical, no-nonsense approach will inspire you to reflect, prioritise, and take meaningful action. Drawing on her wealth of experience, she encourages you to think beyond the clinic room and design a role that truly serves you. A must-read for any dietitian seeking an enjoyable and fulfilling career in private practice."

**Rachel Tutill, APD, Team Leader:
Optimum Intake Dietitians.**

"Jodie's experience and ability to teach concepts to dietitians that actually work is what makes this book so valuable! It's the guide that every new (and even not-so-new) dietitian needs to have to help them thrive in private practice, whether they work for themselves or someone else. It's the missing piece that we don't get at university – because let's be real, not all dietitians want to work in hospitals. From pricing our services to overcoming the mindset issues we need to be successful as dietitians, this book covers all the things we need to succeed. Even as an experienced dietitian, I continue to learn from Jodie's expertise and strongly recommend this book to be on every dietitian's shelf."

Louise Murray, APD

Disclaimer

The content in this book is drawn from my personal experiences, professional insights, and general industry knowledge. It is provided for educational and informational purposes only and should not be considered legal, financial, medical, or personalised business advice. Every business and professional situation is unique. Please consult qualified legal, financial, or other professional advisors before making decisions that may affect your business, career, or personal circumstances.

Dedication

To my husband, our two boys, and my parents—thank you for supporting my ambition, fueling my drive, and believing in every idea and dream I've chased. And to you, the reader, may you always be surrounded by people who believe in you just as fiercely.

Contents

Testimonials	iii
Disclaimer	v
Dedication	vii
Introduction	3
1. Welcome to Private Practice – A Different Kind of Dietetics	7
2. Dietetics Meets Business – The Dietitian Private Practice Framework	19
3. Think Bigger – Let Go of Industry Limiting Beliefs	29
4. Know Your Worth – Charging, Boundaries, and Valuing Your Work	41
5. Understanding Funding – Making Medicare and More Work for You	55
6. Confident Consultation – Structuring Sessions That Work	67
7. From Advice to Action – Planning Treatment That Delivers Results	95
8. Reporting With Impact – Writing Reports That Matter	105
9. Getting the Job – Private Practice Interview Secrets	117
10. Be the Dietitian Practices Want to Keep	135
11. Burnout Isn't Inevitable – Build a Career That Lasts	147
12. Don't Let Your Niche Define You – Grow Your Skills, Not Just Your Title	161
Book Wrap-Up	171
About the Author	173
Offers	177

*'You don't need to feel confident to begin –
begin, and then confidence grows.'*

Introduction

Welcome to the private practice you were never taught about.

If you've ever stepped into private practice feeling underprepared, overwhelmed, or unsure of where to begin, you are not alone.

University taught you the science. Placement gave you a glimpse of the 'real world.' But what no one gave you was the roadmap for turning your dietetic degree into a sustainable, profitable, purpose-driven career.

I wrote this book to change that.

Whether you're fresh out of university or a few years into building your private practice, this book is your permission to stop winging it and start designing a business and career that truly works for you. It's here to fill in the gaps you didn't even know you had, offering practical guidance, mindset shifts, business-savvy tools, and real-world lessons from someone who's been where you are.

I'm Jodie Sheraton. I've been an Accredited Practising Dietitian for over 19 years and have built multiple successful dietetic businesses including Optimum Intake Dietitians, Myrtle Oak Clinic, and Elevated Dietetics. But I didn't start with a clear plan or a bulletproof mindset. Like many, I started with a few part-time gigs, a whole lot of doubt, and a desire to 'be good at something'.

Through trial, error, burnout, and breakthrough, I discovered that being a great dietitian isn't just about knowing your medical nutrition therapy. It's about understanding people, including yourself. It's about systems, boundaries, supervision, and knowing your worth. It's about confidently navigating funding models and feeling empowered to price your services, rather than apologising for them.

This book is a collection of chapters written from lessons I wish I had known earlier and the conversations I've had with hundreds of private practice dietitians I've mentored. Each chapter is designed to be standalone something you can flip to in the moment you need it most and together, they build a complete toolkit for private practice success.

Inside, you'll learn how to:

- Navigate funding models without undercharging or overworking.
- Reframe your mindset and drop the industry limiting beliefs holding you back.
- Build strong boundaries and prevent burnout, yes, even in your early years.
- Become the team member every practice wants to keep, or the leader others want to follow.
- Master the art of delivering consultations, gaining aligned referrals, and feel confident in your communication.

INTRODUCTION

- Interview well, negotiate with clarity, and stand out by being unapologetically yourself.

This isn't a fluff-filled, feel-good read. It's a practical guide for dietitians who want to create a business and career that fuels their lifestyle, honours their values, and grows their impact.

And you don't need to have it all figured out.

You just need to be willing to do things differently.

Welcome to your next step.

Welcome to Private Practice – A Different Kind of Dietetics

'Being a great clinician won't get you over the line if you don't also build your business skillset.'

A different kind of dietetics. Forget what you have learnt about working as a dietitian in a hospital setting, it's no longer relevant or applicable when working in private practice.

Private practice isn't just another job, it's a completely different way of thinking, working, and delivering dietetic care. It's where clinical expertise meets business awareness, creativity, and self-leadership. And yet, most university programs still train dietitians for hospital settings, assuming you'll be working in large teams with structured roles, funding models, and procedures.

So why does this matter?

However, over half of new dietitian graduates are now entering private practice within their first 12 months, often with no training in business, client experience, or service delivery outside of a clinical ward. This mismatch between what you're taught and what the real world requires is not just inconvenient, it's disempowering.

When you enter private practice with only your clinical lens, you might feel confused about pricing, unsure about referrals, anxious about not knowing what's "allowed", and overwhelmed by how different every client is. You might not know how to set boundaries, charge confidently, or even believe that you're capable of running a sustainable service.

But here's the truth: private practice is an incredible opportunity. One that offers not only professional freedom and personal satisfaction, but also the ability to create long-lasting impact, financial success, and career growth that truly aligns with your values.

You deserve to know this from the start, not years down the road after burnout, undercharging, or confusion has taken its toll. You're not broken or behind if you feel unsure. You've just never been shown how private practice works.

And now you will be.

This chapter is your foundation. It will help you:

- Understand how private practice differs from hospital or community work.
- Reframe your expectations so you're not constantly comparing yourself to outdated models.

- Recognise that private practice is learnable, and you're allowed to build your career in your own way.

The goal? To help you see private practice as a legitimate, exciting, and sustainable option for your career, not a fallback plan.

Let's define the key terms that will help you navigate this new professional landscape:

- Private Practice: A work setting where a dietitian operates independently or as part of a business, offering services directly to paying clients (or indirectly through Medicare, private health, or community programs). It often includes administrative tasks, marketing, and ongoing client relationship management.
- Client-Paid Model: Unlike the salaried hospital role, private practice income comes from delivering client services. These can be funded directly or through schemes such as Medicare, NDIS, DVA, or private health. This means clients become your customers and that changes everything about how you serve and communicate.
- Business-Minded Dietitian: A clinician who understands that service delivery, pricing, marketing, documentation, and systems are all part of running a successful practice. You don't need to be "born" a businessperson, you can learn the skills step by step.

Over my many years working as a dietitian and seeing dietitians come and go, many new dietitians have stated "I don't have enough experience to know what I want".

Let me reassure you, it's completely normal. I suggest using reflection to uncover your values, strengths, and preferences. You're not meant to have it all figured out yet, this is part of the learning process. There is no "wrong" starting point. As you gain experience, you'll have more clarity and the ability to pivot, shift focus, or redefine your path as needed.

You likely have more experience than you give yourself credit for: life experience, nutrition knowledge, placement hours, and exposure to different settings. And all of that *is* enough to begin your journey as a dietitian.

There is no set 'experience threshold' beyond being an Accredited Practising Dietitian that determines whether you can work in private practice. Yes, there's a lot to learn, but that shouldn't be the reason you hold back. You only gain experience by *doing*, so start doing your thing!

You're probably thinking, 'Aren't there already too many dietitians in private practice? I won't be able to stand out'.

The number of practicing dietitians is still much lower compared to other allied health professions like physiotherapists or psychologists, there is plenty of room for all of us to grow, collaborate, and thrive rather than compete. We all have our own unique approaches, communication styles, and ways of supporting clients. There is *always* room for more qualified dietitians to be promoting credible nutrition and providing quality care.

I can guarantee this kind of thinking isn't stopping the next 'non-qualified nutrition guru' from launching their own business or spreading false information online so don't let it hold you back either.

The pressure early on in your career can feel daunting, filled with thoughts like, 'I need a full-time job now' or 'private practice can't support me'.

Private practice can start in whatever way you want it to. Many dietitians begin with part-time hours and gradually build up as they gain experience and referrals. There are also options to join established teams rather than going it alone.

You can treat private practice as a side hustle at first. Consulting in the evenings or on weekends is a great way to slowly grow your business without compromising your current income *or* your long-term vision.

It's important to remember that private practice is about building a business. And a lot of dietitians really enjoy helping people, so it's understandable that you may be feeling hesitant or scared and thinking 'I'm not business-minded — I just want to help people'. Private practice calls on both clinical and business skills, but you don't need to have it all figured out from the start. Business skills *can* be learned and the creativity, freedom, and impact of private practice often outweigh the discomfort of the learning curve. Most of us leave university having only experienced hospital placements, where conversations about money or payment never happen. It can feel foreign at first to place a dollar value on your work, promote your services, or attract paying clients. That's normal. The good news? These are skills and we'll be building them together. Throughout this book, you'll explore mindset shifts and new ways of thinking that will help you stay client-focused *while also* making strong, confident, and values-based business decisions.

Let me share with you some of the many benefits to building a career in private practice.

Making money will be your freedom.

Owning your own private practice gives you control and responsibility over your income. You're not locked into a fixed award rate, nor do you need to wait for permission to earn more. When you learn how to package, price, and communicate your services effectively, you unlock financial independence and that's what gives you choices in your career, lifestyle, and legacy. However, there is no guarantee that clients will keep coming, referrals will continue, or your pay will be consistent. The responsibility to keep generating money can feel stressful but either way, it's up to you. The financial outcome of your business is what you make it, if you're willing to keep moving forward.

Freedom to design your schedule and services.

Want to work three long days and take Fridays off? Prefer working with groups instead of individuals? Want to offer walk-in consults or telehealth from home? In private practice, you get to decide what your work week looks like. This flexibility allows you to work in a way that honours your energy, strengths, and priorities. There will be seasons where you need to invest more time, energy, or resources, especially during periods of growth or change, but the beauty is that the choice is yours. Learning to value and protect your time will help you maintain the kind of schedule you want.

Greater adaptability and creative freedom in how you practice.

Unlike the rigid protocols often found in hospital settings, private practice invites creativity. You can trial new approaches, tailor your methods, create your own client tools, build programs, run workshops, the opportunities are endless. You can evolve your practice alongside your interests and your clients' changing needs. If something flops, no sweat, just reflect, pivot, adapt, and move forward. Every experiment teaches you something valuable that you'll carry into the next phase of your work.

Opportunity to build deep client relationships across time.

In hospital settings, you might only see a patient once before discharge. In private practice, you can follow a client's journey over weeks, months, or even years. You'll witness their growth, adjust plans in real-time, and become a trusted partner in their progress. These relationships are deeply fulfilling, and they often lead to strong word-of-mouth referrals from clients who want others to experience what you've helped them achieve.

Capacity to build a thriving team or join one that aligns with your values.

Whether your future lies in leadership or collaboration, private practice allows you to shape your environment. You might build your own team and create a workplace culture you love or join an existing clinic whose mission aligns with your own. The key is remembering that private practice doesn't have to be lonely. Your team might sit in the room next door or connect with you from afar over Zoom. Either way, the opportunity to feel part of something bigger is always available.

It's been incredible to observe a huge shift in the industry, with over 50% of dietitians now entering private practice post-graduation — more than those going into hospital settings. Yet, university training still doesn't prepare dietitians for it adequately. Research based on multiple industry surveys has shown that more than two-thirds of private practice dietitian business owners earn less than if they worked in the hospital setting and their income is below minimum wage for a health professional.

The solution to fixing this? Building better business skills. There are no other reasons why dietitians can't build a sustainable and financially rewarding career out of private practice. If other allied health professionals are building group practices with long-term success, then dietitians can too, but dietitians won't unless they learn the skills to succeed in business.

> *'Private practice is a business; it needs to make money to be sustainable and support your career long-term.'*

Let me share with you how I started in private practice as a new graduate.

I began my private practice in 2007 with a $2,000 loan from my parents. That loan paid for the essentials: a laptop, a Yellow Pages ad (before websites were common or affordable), and a portable set of scales. My first clients were seen in their homes; I didn't even have a clinic room. At the same time, I was working multiple casual positions, one in a hospital as a paediatric dietitian (hired from my university placement experience), a research assistant at the University of Newcastle, where I studied and I was involved in a rotation of wards/roles within another large hospital. This casual nature, with a broad range of experiences, lasted up to two years. Then I applied for a two-day per week public health dietitian position in an early intervention eating disorder role. It was a dynamic position with generous professional development opportunities, access to frequent supervision, and collaboration with psychologists and mental health professionals.

I genuinely loved the work, which is why it took nearly 10 years to shift into full-time private practice. It wasn't a lack of readiness; it was passion and commitment. It was also the spark I needed to start my second private practice, one where I could utilise my eating disorder expertise and skills and increase access to specialised care within my local community. This was the creation of Myrtle Oak Clinic. Over time, I built my private practice businesses steadily. I offered services in GP clinics, aged care facilities, gyms, specialist clinics, and rented our own clinic room space. Eventually, I transitioned into leadership, managing a growing team of clinicians and administration officers.

That growth brought a new challenge: developing business and leadership skills. I began investing in coaches and mentors, but I often found that the advice was based on models used by physiotherapists and speech pathologists. Their service structures, pricing strategies, and workflows didn't apply to dietitians as easily. Their ways of working didn't align with how dietetic services are best delivered. So, I began designing my own methods. With the support of my team, we created a private practice model that was financially sustainable, values-driven, and effective. This book shares what we learned along the way, so that you don't have to reinvent the wheel.

There's no one way to practice.

If you're reading this book, chances are you've already imagined how you'd like to work with clients. That vision matters.

Being a dietitian in private practice is not about fitting into a single mould. You'll develop your own methods, communication style, and client approach. There are frameworks and best practices, yes, but how you bring those to life will be unique to you.

Our dietitian positions have evolved and over time have included everything from toddler food play therapy to aged care home visits, telehealth consultations, supermarket tours, and community expos. No two days look the same. And no two dietitians practice in the same way, even when working with the same client group.

This diversity is what makes our profession stronger. In private practice, flexibility within a clinical framework is essential. The way we deliver education, run our sessions, and connect with clients in this setting is different from how it's done in hospitals. That's why this book includes adaptable templates and tools designed to help you find your own rhythm, not follow a script. Use what fits, tweak what doesn't, and keep evolving.

The power of joining a team.

Private practice isn't just for entrepreneurs who want to own the business, it's for dietitians who want to connect with clients in a special way that is unique to the private setting. You can have that not only as a business owner, but also as a team member within someone else's business. And quite frankly, it might be nice to leave all that business stress to the owner, or perhaps for a stage later in your career! I spent years working across the public health system and within multiple hospital teams, some empowering, others not so much. These experiences helped shape my vision for a private practice that was different. One where dietitians new to private practice wouldn't feel unsupported and alone.

Today, our team offers structured onboarding, paid training, supervision, and support. New dietitians join a values-led culture where systems are in place and help is always within reach. This kind of workplace is only possible because the business is financially healthy because fees are set to support both clients and team members, and because leadership decisions are made with intention.

Not every private practice has these supports. But even in smaller or newer clinics, you can make a difference. Bring ideas, contribute to building systems, and add value to the business you're part of. Being employed in private practice allows you to focus on client work, grow your skills, and gain confidence, without the pressure of business ownership.

And when the time comes to move on or start your own practice, do it with transparency and integrity. Review your contract, understand the boundaries around client contact and referrals, and speak openly with your manager. Protect your reputation, and you'll carry that goodwill into the next stage of your career.

Before you move onto the next chapter, I encourage you to reflect on these two questions:

1. Why is private practice appealing to you and what excites you about it?
2. Write down what a sustainable, values-aligned private practice career could look like for you.

Dietetics Meets Business – The Dietitian Private Practice Framework

Private practice success doesn't happen by accident, it happens at the intersection of clinical excellence, positive client experiences, and business mastery.

As dietitians you are familiar with the term 'Clinical Skills'. The foundational nutrition knowledge, counselling ability, critical thinking, and evidence-based practice dietitians apply to support clients in achieving their health goals. While essential, clinical skills alone are not enough to sustain a thriving private practice, they must work in harmony with business skills and client experience delivery.

So, what am I referring to when I use the term 'Client Experience'? It's the full journey your client has from first contact to final session, including how they book, how they are welcomed, what they receive during sessions, how they are followed up with, and how communication is handled throughout. A strong client experience increases trust, compliance, and referrals.

You could categorise the elements of the client experience under business skills, however I like to give greater emphasis to its importance, so I will use it as its own area of focus. Business skills are the operational, financial, marketing, and leadership capabilities needed to run a successful and sustainable private practice. This includes managing time, money, services, systems, and people with clarity and confidence.

The Private Practice Framework is what integrates clinical skills, business skills, and client experience strategies to hit the "success sweet spot".

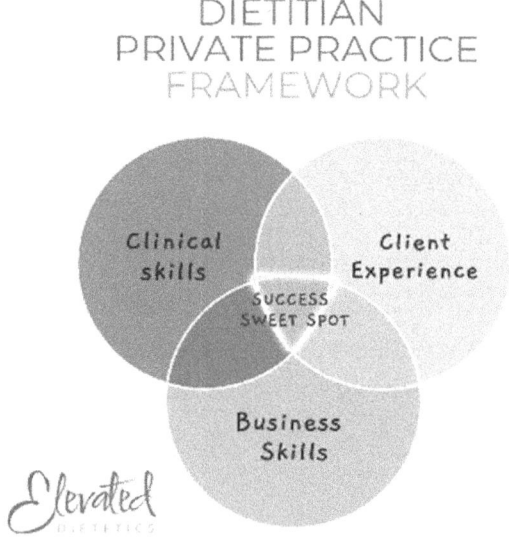

Image 1. The Dietitian Private Practice Framework.

Many dietitians enter private practice with strong clinical training but little-to-no preparation for the business world. While they eagerly invest in clinical professional development, they often ignore the essential areas of client experience and business skills that truly sustain and grow a private practice.

Without those foundations in place, it's no surprise that burnout, undercharging, inconsistent referrals, and low confidence become common. It's not because they aren't a good enough dietitian. It's because they haven't been taught the business and client experience skills that make private practice sustainable and profitable.

Private practice isn't about choosing between being a caring dietitian and being a capable business owner. It's about learning how to integrate both. You *can* be values-driven *and* financially stable. You *can* deliver exceptional client care *and* build a profitable business that works for you.

When you focus only on clinical skills, you may stay stuck in a cycle of under-earning, working late into the night, and questioning whether private practice is worth it. When you develop your client experience and business capabilities, you reclaim time, increase your income, grow your confidence, and the ability to serve more of the right people, without burning out.

This chapter will help you:

- Shift your mindset from "just a clinician" to empowered practitioner-business owner.
- Understand the three key pillars of success in private practice.

- Begin to implement the elements of *The Private Practice Framework* into your own practice.

> *'You didn't get taught this at university,
> but you can absolutely learn it now.'*

The Dietitian Private Practice Framework

At the heart of this chapter and of everything I teach at Elevated Dietetics, is a simple but powerful concept: private practice success happens where three essential skillsets intersect.

These three areas; Clinical Skills, Business Skills, and Client Experience, form the foundation of the Dietitian Private Practice Framework.

In Image 1, you'll see a Venn diagram with three overlapping circles. The middle is where these three pillars meet — that's your *success sweet spot*.

Let's break down why each circle matters:

- Clinical Skills ensure you're delivering accurate, evidence-based, and compassionate care.
- Business Systems keep your practice running smoothly, sustainably, and profitably.
- Client Experience makes your service memorable, impactful, and referral-worthy.

You may start your journey stronger in one area than the others and that's okay. The magic happens when you intentionally grow and balance all three. Many dietitians start strong clinically but hit burnout or stagnation without business systems or a great client journey. Others may run their business efficiently but struggle to retain clients because the experience isn't there yet.

The Dietitian Private Practice Framework acts as a diagnostic tool and a map. It shows you what you're already doing well and where you might focus your energy next. I want this framework to become a recognised standard in our profession, something dietitians can refer to again and again as they grow their practices, onboard new team members, or refine their services.

It's not about being perfect in every area all the time. It's about becoming aware of the gaps, building your confidence, and creating a private practice that serves both your clients and *you*.

Before we move forward, let's address one of the most common fears that holds dietitians back from stepping fully into private practice, the fear of not being business-minded. It doesn't need to be your strength, yet—business is a skillset like any other. You didn't enter your degree knowing how to write a nutrition care plan or interpret bloods, and you learned those with time, support, and structure. The same applies here. You don't need to do it alone, and you certainly don't need to figure it out through trial and error. With the right coaching and resources, especially those tailored for dietitians, you can grow your business confidence just like you've grown your clinical skills.

And as you begin building your business skillset, one of the first and most confronting areas you'll likely face is money. Feeling uncomfortable talking about money, charging clients and taking a payment. This makes complete sense, and I'll tell you why. Most of us weren't exposed to conversations about money during our training. But here's the truth: when you avoid talking about money, you risk undercharging, overworking, and confusing your clients. Learning how to confidently and transparently discuss your fees not only helps you feel more grounded, but it also builds trust with your clients. It shows them that you value your work, and in turn, it invites them to value it too.

It's confronting to think that you can have the best clinical skills in the world, but if no one knows about you or understands the value of what you offer, your business won't thrive.

> *'Business systems are what gets them in the door—client experience and clinical skills are what keeps the doors open.'*

To help you see what this looks like in real life, let's look at three different stories of dietitians at different stages of private practice. You might see yourself in one or all of them. Each one illustrates how applying business skills and client experience strategies can lead to meaningful and sustainable change.

The Overwhelmed New Graduate: Lily

Fresh out of university, Lily poured hours into writing detailed meal plans and typing notes late into the night, yet she was still worried she wasn't doing enough. Despite her best clinical effort, clients dropped off after just one or two sessions. Together we reflected on her work week and identified that she was not sticking to her session time, often going over, and doing extra post-session work without charging for it. This snowballed into late-night admin and ongoing stress.

Lily had evidence that people were referring to her, but her session structure was letting her down. With some simple changes she began to track her time, broke down her services into fee-based offerings, simplified her follow-up systems, invested in an AI note-taking program, and used client onboarding templates, and everything changed. She halved her admin load, got paid for all her time and services, improved client outcomes, and started to enjoy her work again.

The Burned-Out Solo Dietitian: Sienna

After five years in private practice, Sienna was exhausted. Her schedule was full, but her bank account wasn't. She resisted getting help because she felt she couldn't afford it. With the brave step of investing in a couple of strategy sessions, we reviewed her service structure and calculated her actual hourly rate — how much was landing in her pocket after expenses. It was clear she needed to increase her fees.

Together we developed a six-month financial plan that included two structured fee increases and a communication strategy to support her existing clients. The plan also included bringing on a part-time admin assistant. That hire was a turning point. It allowed Sienna to stay focused on her higher-value work as a dietitian and offered another person the opportunity to deliver excellent client service through admin support. No longer stuck in $10 tasks, she could now focus on $1,000 tasks and serve her clients with renewed passion. For the first time in years, Sienna took a real holiday without worrying about her clients or cash flow.

The Dietitian Who Avoided Business Altogether: Kelly

Kelly knew she was great with clients but avoided anything 'businessy'. Her fees were inconsistent, she undercharged, and marketing felt overwhelming. Then she joined the Elevated Dietetics business coaching program, which is a program designed specifically for dietitians in private practice who are ready to grow but don't know how to take the next leap.

With the right tools and support, she reconnected to her core purpose and identified exactly who she wanted to support. She rebranded, clarified her service structure, ensured her pricing was consistent and reflective of value, and developed a messaging strategy she could confidently use in communications and marketing. Within six months, she had automated key business functions, implemented reliable report templates, and hired her first team member.

Each of these dietitians had to make challenging decisions and take bold actions within their business to see the improvements they were hoping for. All dietitians want to be able to do a few key things.

Build a sustainable, profitable business they love.

When you integrate solid systems and pricing strategies, your business becomes financially viable and emotionally rewarding. You're no longer guessing your way through — it becomes intentional, clear, and tailored to how *you* want to work. A well-run business supports your ability to deliver value to clients, invest in better resources, and continuously improve the client experience. Having satisfied clients is how you build both sustainability and profitability.

Increasing client satisfaction and retention leads to more referrals.

Happy clients are repeat clients, and they tell their friends. When you deliver consistent, high-quality experiences from onboarding to final session, you build trust and improve outcomes. That leads to loyalty, longevity, and word-of-mouth referrals. If your clients find it difficult to book in, face confusing payment processes, or leave sessions overwhelmed and unsupported, they're unlikely to come back or refer others. Place yourself in their shoes and start making customer-friendly improvements to ensure their experience is seamless, engaging, and worth returning to.

Attract the right clients and opportunities aligned with your values.

When your services and communication reflect who you are and what matters to you, you'll naturally attract people who resonate with your work. This means better outcomes, stronger rapport, and a more fulfilling practice. It also means learning when to say no. Not every opportunity is the right one. Don't let unaligned offers drain your time and energy, protect your capacity for the clients and projects that light you up.

Feel confident charging what you're worth.

Pricing becomes less scary when you understand your value and can clearly communicate it. When your fees reflect your skills, effort, and impact, clients respect your service, and you stop undervaluing yourself. Most people have no idea what your business costs are or what you earn. If someone says your fees are too high, reflect on all you provide, look at your numbers, and stand firm in your pricing. Educate clients on the value they're receiving. And if it's not the right fit, be prepared to refer them to someone who may better suit their budget. You don't need to serve everyone, just the ones who understand the value you offer.

Learning more about nutrition won't fix your lack of clients, poor cash flow, or burnout.

Learning business will.

Imagine what would happen if dietitians viewed their business with the same level of care and planning as they do for their clinical skills? What would happen if learning business skills felt empowering, not overwhelming? What if improving client experience became the fastest way to grow your referrals? What if you could work less, earn more, and make a bigger impact, all at the same time?

> What I want you to do as an outcome from this chapter is to:
>
> 1. Start treating business skills as essential not optional for private practice success.
> 2. Identify one area in your client experience that could be improved (e.g., onboarding, session flow, communication, or follow-up).
> 3. Explore support or coaching that aligns with your values and practice goals, don't go it alone.

Think Bigger – Let Go of Industry Limiting Beliefs

The biggest barriers in private practice often aren't financial, clinical, or logistical, they're the beliefs we carry about what's possible.

Far too many private practice dietitians are unknowingly operating under outdated beliefs passed down from university lecturers, hospital mentors, or fellow clinicians who never ran a successful business themselves. These beliefs are often accepted as "truth" simply because they're widespread — not because they're true.

You may have heard them whispered early in your career:

- *'You should work in a hospital first before working in private practice.'*
- *'You can't charge more, clients won't pay.'*

- *'Dietitians shouldn't focus on money; it's about helping people.'*
- *'Private practice isn't stable or secure, it's a side hustle at best.'*

These statements aren't innocent advice, they're inherited fear. And when left unchallenged, they become powerful constraints.

The cost of these beliefs is high. They cause dietitians to:

- Undercharge for their time and expertise
- Take on too many clients, leading to burnout
- Say yes to misaligned opportunities out of fear
- Avoid business growth out of guilt or imposter syndrome
- Limit their career paths and income potential

But even more damaging than the financial consequences is what these beliefs do to your *confidence*. They quietly erode your sense of worth, your ability to lead, and your capacity to innovate.

You might find yourself hesitating to raise fees, delaying launching a new offer, doubting your niche, or comparing yourself to others who seem 'more qualified' all because of beliefs that were never yours to begin with.

These aren't your thoughts, they're hand-me-downs. And it's time to return them. Because here's the truth: private practice *can* be a financially sustainable, personally fulfilling, and deeply impactful career. But only if you give yourself permission to believe it's possible.

And permission doesn't come from a boss, a textbook, or a peer-reviewed article. It comes from you.

By recognising and reframing your limiting beliefs, you not only give yourself permission to grow, you become part of a movement that reshapes the identity of dietitians in business.

You stop asking *'Can I?'* and start declaring *'Watch me'*.

Every private practice dietitian encounters moments of doubt. It's normal. But left unchallenged, those doubts harden into beliefs that quietly limit your choices. Below are some of the most common objections I've heard and the truth-based reframes that will help you move forward with confidence.

First let's get clear on the language:

- Limiting Beliefs: Internalised thoughts or societal messages that hold you back from pursuing your goals. *Example: 'I'm not experienced enough to charge that much'.*
- Imposter Syndrome: The persistent fear of being exposed as a fraud, despite evidence of your competence and value.
- Reframing: The practice of identifying unhelpful thoughts and replacing them with empowering, truth-based perspectives.

'I'm not experienced enough to grow a successful business.'

Experience helps, but it's not the deciding factor. What matters more is how you show up: with clarity in your offer, confidence in your message, and a willingness to learn and adapt.

You don't need years of working in a hospital setting to succeed in private practice, actually lots of dietitians who take the leap from hospital to private practice with honed clinical skills still feel stuck when it comes to elements of the client experience and business skills, what you need is direction.

Many successful practice owners launched their businesses early in their careers, not because they had *all the answers*, but because they were willing to ask the right questions, take smart risks, and seek mentorship. Experience is gained by doing, not waiting.

If you're reading this chapter, you're already ahead of most. You're learning, growing, and choosing to lead with intention. And that's exactly how successful businesses are built.

'I feel guilty charging for healthcare.'

This belief is one of the most damaging and most deeply ingrained. It's tied to the idea that making money and making a difference are at odds. But they're not. Helping people *and* being well-compensated for your time, energy, and expertise isn't unethical, it's sustainable. You're not charging for *healthcare itself*, you're charging for the hours you've studied, the emotional bandwidth you hold, the personalised advice you give, and the transformation you help create. This is *quality income* earned through compassion and competence. If you undercharge out of guilt, you risk depleting the very resources you need to continue showing up for others.

Making money from helping people isn't greedy.

It's what allows you to keep helping. The cost of living is always on the rise and us dietitians are not exempt from this financial impact. Business expenses are the highest they have ever been, and we need to be making a profit to keep our business growing and thriving so we can continue showing up for our clients.

When you shed the outdated stories and choose to think bigger, the transformation reaches far beyond your mindset it reshapes your business, your career, and your identity as a dietitian.

Here's what becomes possible when you break free from limiting beliefs:

Develop the confidence to charge what you're worth.

No more second-guessing your pricing or discounting your services out of fear. Instead, set fees based on factual financial figures and add extra for the *value you provide*, not guilt and back them with professionalism and clarity. Charging what you're worth doesn't just support your income, it signals to your clients (and to yourself) that your work matters and deserves respect. Confident pricing isn't about being greedy, it's about creating a sustainable business that serves both you and your clients well long term.

Overcome imposter syndrome with practical mindset tools.

Feeling like a fraud when you're actually competent is exhausting and more common than you think. This work helps you identify when imposter thoughts show up, why they're there, and how to reframe them into grounded confidence. You'll stop waiting to 'feel ready' and start building the evidence that you already are.

Mindset isn't fluff, it's the foundation that supports every business decision you make.

Do you see unqualified nutrition 'gurus' or 'influencers' crippled by imposter syndrome? No, they stand in their convictions, speak with authority and gain trust and followers by communicating with confidence. Now, don't get me wrong, I don't condone promoting misinformation, but what we can learn from these people is that if we're able to show up with confidence—backed by informed science and evidence—we could take over misinformation out in the world if we could just remove or move past the mindset hurdles dietitians often experience.

Create a career path uniquely suited to your values and strengths.

Private practice is not one-size-fits-all. When you think bigger, you stop trying to mimic what others are doing and start designing a career that aligns with *your* vision, whether that means running a solo practice, building a team, creating digital programs, speaking or mentoring, or something entirely new.

You didn't become a dietitian to follow a script. You became one to make a difference in a way that feels authentic to you. Don't be held back by what others believe you should do next, you can determine your next steps, seek input from those you aspire to be like, or who are a few steps ahead in the direction you wish to venture. Ultimately you are in the driver seat of your own career pathway.

Let me share with you some shocking industry truths:

Recent workforce research paints a very clear picture with 77% of business owners reported feeling a strong sense of accomplishment, only 38% felt adequately remunerated for their work, and just 37% agreed they received adequate support in their role.

Perhaps most concerning, 35% of business owners acknowledged feeling unwell due to stress in their business.

This highlights what many of us already know: passion and purpose are not enough on their own to sustain a long-term career in private practice. Without the right systems, mentoring, and business skills, stress can undermine even the most dedicated clinicians.

Recruitment and retention challenges are also front of mind for practice owners. The study showed that many were dissatisfied with both the number and quality of applications for mid-career roles (5–10 years' experience), while finding it somewhat easier to recruit new graduates. Yet, onboarding and supervising staff was described as one of the greatest workforce challenges, requiring both time and financial resources. Owners spoke of the disruption caused by team changes and the fine balance between meeting client demand and supporting staff to grow without burning out.

These findings don't just highlight individual struggles—they reflect the systemic realities of private practice. The truth is, confidence in business skills, sustainable structures, and intentional mentoring aren't optional extras; they're essential to the health of our profession and the clients we serve.

These numbers remind us that the challenges are real—but they don't have to define us. Letting go of industry-limiting beliefs isn't a one-time event it's an ongoing practice. But each time you choose a new story, you're not just changing your own future. You're showing every dietitian watching you that it's possible for them too.*

Let's look at some more examples of dietitians doing just this:

The Bold Leap

When Emily graduated from university, she was passionate about women's hormone health but everywhere she turned, the advice was the same: *'Start in a hospital first. Get experience. Don't go too niche too early.'*

But Emily couldn't shake the feeling that she was ready now and that her unique interests were a strength, not a liability. So, instead of taking a 'safe' job that didn't light her up, she launched her own practice right out of graduation. She chose a specific niche she genuinely cared about, invested in private practice mentorship, and surrounded herself with a community that encouraged growth over fear. She didn't have all the answers, but she did have clarity and support.

---

* Kirkegaard A, Wright O, Clark P, Ball L. *Development and baseline findings of a national dataset describing Australian private practice dietetics.* Nutrition & Dietetics. 2025;1–9. doi:10.1111/1747-0080.70027

She got clear on her service offerings, pricing, and messaging. She showed up consistently online, built genuine connections with her audience, and spoke to a need that was being underserved in her area. Within the first year, she had a waitlist. People weren't turned off by her being 'new', they were drawn to her passion, her professionalism, and her ability to speak directly to their needs.

What others saw as a risk, Emily saw as alignment.

And that alignment became the foundation of a business built on authenticity, courage, and impact. There were both client experience skills and business skills that she developed along the way and Emily was not hesitant to take risks and try new things, things that she felt her clients would really benefit from having in their treatment plans. Emily had to get comfortable with charging for her niche services and was thrilled when the momentum started to pick up from word-of-mouth referrals.

The Rewrite

Sarah had been in private practice for almost eight years. She was experienced, skilled, and deeply committed to her clients, but her business was running her, not the other way around. She booked every client herself. She answered every email. She took on admin tasks after hours, worked weekends to "catch up", and prided herself on being a one-woman powerhouse.

Underneath it all was a belief she didn't even realise she held: *'I have to do it all myself to earn success.'*

Eventually, the cracks began to show — in her energy, in her family life, and in her health. The joy she once had for dietetics was fading, replaced by resentment and exhaustion.

During a coaching session, she was asked one powerful question: *'What if being successful didn't mean doing everything yourself?'*

That question led to a mindset shift and a practical change. Sarah hired a part-time admin assistant. She let go of control, delegated tasks that didn't need her skillset, and started creating space in her week to work *on* her business, not just *in* it.

Within a year, she had:

- Doubled her income
- Reduced her working hours by nearly 30%
- Rekindled her creativity and drive

Her business didn't just grow, *she* grew. And in doing so, she rewrote the story of what success could look like: collaborative, supported, and sustainable.

From Burnout to Belief

Michael had been in private practice for over a decade. Clients loved him. He was kind, patient, knowledgeable and always willing to go the extra mile. But behind the scenes, he was struggling. His rates hadn't changed in three years. He often discounted his services when clients 'couldn't afford it'. He'd add unpaid extras like emails, meal plans, and extended sessions because he didn't want to seem greedy. He told himself this was part of being caring and ethical, but deep down, he was tired. He was working long hours for limited income, and his own wellbeing was suffering.

One day, in a coaching session I asked him: *'Do you think your clients would still value your care if you valued yourself more?'*

That question stuck with him. Michael sat down and did a true cost-of-service breakdown, the time, the overheads, the unpaid hours. What he found was shocking: he was essentially being paid less than a casual retail worker. It was time to honour his value.

He raised his fees, not astronomically, but enough to reflect his experience, expertise, and energy. He communicated the change clearly to his clients, offering them context and confidence in the continued quality of his service.

And something surprising happened, almost every client stayed. And with the added income, Michael began to enjoy his business again. He worked fewer hours, took better care of himself, and showed up more fully for the people he served. He realised that caring for others didn't have to come at the cost of himself and that believing in his worth was the first step in building a business that could last.

Transformation starts with action. Below are three simple but powerful steps to begin rewriting your story.

1. Identify one limiting belief you've been holding and rewrite it.
2. Write your own "I am" statement that reflects your value, skills, and vision.
3. Have one bold conversation this week, whether it's about raising fees, saying no, or pitching your service with confidence.

Know Your Worth – Charging, Boundaries, and Valuing Your Work

Private practice isn't just about helping people; it's about building a business that helps you thrive too.

Far too many private practice dietitians are unsure of how to charge, how to say no, or how to stand firm in their professional value. They may have left university with exceptional clinical knowledge but not the mindset or tools needed to set fees, communicate boundaries, or protect their energy in the real world of business.

When you don't know your worth, you become vulnerable to burnout and boundary erosion. You find yourself undercharging, overdelivering, and constantly questioning whether you're doing enough. Without clear pricing and boundaries, your private practice can slowly turn into something that drains you, rather than supports you.

Knowing your worth means having a deep understanding of what it costs to run your business, the value your services provide, and the impact you make in your clients' lives. It's about moving beyond vague feelings of 'charging what you're worth' and grounding your decisions in real numbers and real results. Thriving in private practice isn't about hustle or comparison, it's about creating a business that is sustainable, profitable, and aligned with your lifestyle and values. And boundaries are what make that possible. They are the structure that protects your energy, your time, and your financial wellbeing, ensuring you can continue doing the work you love without burning out or selling yourself short. Together, these elements are the foundation of a career and a business that works for you.

That's why boundaries matter.

Other boundaries that are important:

- Time Boundaries: Working past your limits, saying yes to "just one more" appointment, or checking emails after hours leads to resentment and exhaustion.
- Communication Boundaries: Allowing clients to message you across multiple platforms at any time erodes clarity and can cause anxiety.
- Clinical Boundaries: Taking on cases outside your scope or continuing to see clients who are no longer progressing is not a sign of dedication, it's a disservice to both of you.
- Disclosure Boundaries: Oversharing personal stories or trying to relate by giving away too much of yourself

can blur the lines between therapeutic connection and emotional over-investment.
- 'Yes' boundaries: Being the reliable one who always says yes might feel helpful, but when it comes at the expense of your own values or workload, it's self-sabotaging.

And of course, there's financial boundaries, the foundation of a sustainable business. This means knowing how to set your fees, sticking to them, charging for your time, and having cancellation and no-show policies that you actually enforce. They inform people of how to work with you, how to respect you, and how seriously you take your profession. When you have clear boundaries, you build a practice that protects your time, your energy, and your livelihood, so you can keep showing up with clarity and care.

You didn't enter this profession to feel anxious about sending invoices or guilty about needing a break. You're here to help people but not at the cost of your own wellbeing or sustainability.

You can help people *and* charge appropriately.
You can set boundaries *and* be respected.
You can value your work *and* expect others to do the same.

Let's start building that version of your business now.

This chapter is going to help you undertake a mindset shift to get you feeling confident about your value your worth and taking steps to level up your mindset.

How to Calculate a Sustainable Fee

You didn't go into private practice to run a charity. You started this journey to make a meaningful impact *and* earn a sustainable income. That starts with knowing your numbers.

Too many dietitians set their fees based on what others are charging, what Medicare or NDIS rebates cover, or what simply 'feels fair'. But guesswork isn't a business strategy, it's a recipe for burnout and resentment.

A Simple Formula to Get Started

Here's a basic equation to calculate your minimum sustainable hourly rate:

(Total Annual Business Expenses + Desired Salary + Entitlements + Profit Buffer) ÷ Billable Hours = Hourly Rate

Let's break that down:

- Total Business Expenses: Software, admin time, insurance, supervision, subscriptions, rent, CPD, equipment, memberships, every cost that keeps your business running.
- Desired Salary: What you want to pay yourself each year (including-tax).
- Entitlements: Budget for holidays, sick days, superannuation, and professional development.
- Profit Buffer: A 10–20% cushion to reinvest in your business or cover unexpected costs.

- Billable Hours: The number of client-facing hours you can realistically deliver. (Hint: it's rarely 40 hours per week; a sustainable estimate is 20–25 hours per week for approximately 44 working weeks per year to account for public holidays, sick days and annual leave.)

What Are You *Really* Earning Per Hour?

Now that you've calculated your minimum hourly rate, take it a step further. Divide that rate by the total number of hours you actually work in a week, not just client consults, but also admin, marketing, supervision, emails, meetings, content creation, and everything else that supports your practice.

This gives you a clearer picture of what you're *really* earning per hour. For most dietitians, it's less than expected and it's often why burnout creeps in unnoticed.

When you look honestly at the numbers, the truth becomes clear: You're not overcharging. You're finally charging what's required to run a viable business. If the numbers feel uncomfortable or too low, that's your signal to adjust, not your cue to work harder for less.

But There's More Than Just Cost: Pricing for *Value*

Now that you've calculated your sustainable base fee, it's time to consider something even more powerful: the value transformation component.

This is the part of your pricing that reflects not just what your service *costs*, but what it *delivers*.

Your base fee covers your time, expenses, and income—the financial minimum for staying afloat. But your *value component* captures what makes your service exceptional. And it allows for pricing variation between different services you may be offering in your practice.

That's what allows you to thrive.

What Your Fee Really Covers, Beyond Time Spent

Your clients aren't just paying for 50 minutes of your time. They're investing in a trusted professional who helps them change their health trajectory.

Here's what your fee truly includes:

- The years of training and CPD you've invested in
- The emotional labour and relational work it takes to build trust
- The resources, templates, and systems that improve their experience
- The tailored strategies and insights you offer beyond the session
- The ripple effect of your work — better health, confidence, habits, and wellbeing

You're not just delivering information. You're offering insight, safety, and transformation. That is worth something.

Adding the Value Margin

There's no right or wrong number here, this is about what feels right for *you* and your business. You might choose to add a 10–25% (or more) margin above your base rate to reflect the transformation you deliver. This is the shift from 'just covering costs' to building a business that thrives, one that supports leave, reinvestment, team growth, and long-term sustainability.

Charging with Confidence: Quick Tips

- ✓ Know your numbers. Don't price based on guesswork or comparison. Calculate your minimum sustainable rate and build from there.
- ✓ Charge for your time. Reports, email consults, group education, and supervision are valuable services—include them in your pricing model.
- ✓ Set and enforce boundaries. A cancellation fee isn't about punishment. It protects your time and teaches clients to respect your schedule.
- ✓ Communicate clearly. Confidently explain your pricing during the first session and include it in your intake and welcome materials.
- ✓ Review regularly. Inflation, business growth, and increased expertise mean your fees should evolve over time. Review them at least annually.

Here's what becomes possible when you stop undervaluing your work and start owning your space in private practice:

Increased confidence in communicating your value.
One of the most important skills you'll develop in private practice is the ability to clearly and confidently articulate your value and it starts with how you talk about your services, pricing, and policies. At first, these conversations might feel clunky or awkward (especially if you're worried about being judged or sounding 'salesy'), but with practice, structure, and the right language, they become second nature. When you speak about your fees with clarity and conviction, you help clients feel secure in their investment and set the tone for a professional, respectful relationship.

A practice that supports, not sacrifices, your life.
You didn't start a business to feel burnt out, underpaid, and resentful. But that's exactly what happens when you undervalue your services or work outside your limits. When you charge appropriately and design your services to align with your energy, values, and goals, your practice becomes something that fits into your life, not something that takes over it. Whether it's flexible hours, boundaries around availability, or choosing clients who energise you, your business should reflect the life you want to live. The more your business supports *you*, the more you can sustainably support others.

Freedom from guilt-driven decision making.
Saying no can feel scary. Setting boundaries such as enforcing cancellation policies, or setting session timing alarms, can feel selfish. But building a sustainable business means learning to make decisions from a place of alignment, not guilt or fear. People-pleasing might feel like the 'nice' thing to do, but it often leads to overextension, undercharging, and inner resentment. When you begin making choices that honour your time, energy, and values,

you reclaim your power and show up with integrity. You'll discover that discomfort fades but clarity and confidence last. You're not being difficult, you're being intentional.

Improved client experience and outcomes.
Clients thrive in environments where expectations are clear, communication is consistent, and the practitioner is confident, grounded, and fully present. Your boundaries, your pricing, your structure these aren't obstacles to care. They *are* part of the care. When your policies are clear, your energy is protected, and your mindset is strong, your clients receive better outcomes because you can show up fully and consistently. When you feel valued and respected, you're able to create that same experience for every client who walks through your door.

But this isn't just theory it plays out in real-life practice, every single day. The way you communicate your fees, hold your boundaries, and design your sessions directly shapes how clients experience your care. Let's look at a few stories that illustrate how learning to value your work and yourself can lead to clearer communication, stronger client relationships, and more sustainable business outcomes. These are examples of what it looks like when dietitians step into their worth and the ripple effects that follow.

Rewriting the Rules – Communication Boundaries in Practice.
Sophie was a compassionate, energetic new dietitian who prided herself on being available and responsive. She genuinely cared about her clients and wanted them to always feel supported. But after only eight months in private practice, she found herself completely overwhelmed. Clients were messaging her on Instagram, texting her appointment questions on Sundays, and sending food diaries at 9pm the night before sessions, expecting a

reply. She didn't want to seem rude or unhelpful, so she responded to everything.

It wasn't long before she dreaded opening her phone. Her work-life boundaries blurred, and the anxiety of being 'always on' started affecting her sleep and her enthusiasm for the job. She felt trapped by her own kindness.

Together, we mapped out her communication policy. We wrote clear, respectful scripts for her to use in client handbooks and appointment confirmations: all appointment communication would go through the clinic email, messages would be responded to within two business days, and social media accounts were not monitored for client contact.

She updated her intake forms, created an email autoresponder, and built the boundaries into her onboarding template. To her surprise, clients adapted quickly and a few even thanked her for the clarity. Sophie felt a wave of relief and professionalism. Her boundaries didn't disconnect her from clients, they deepened the sense of structure and trust in the working relationship.

A Lunch Break Changed Everything – Time Boundaries That Protect You

Michael was a solo dietitian running back-to-back sessions, skipping breaks, and staying up late writing notes. He thought working hard would equal helping more people. But instead, his sessions started feeling rushed, his patience wore thin, and he constantly worried about burnout. His friends and family barely saw him, and the passion he once had was slipping away.

He realised his calendar was running *him* not the other way around.

We started by blocking 15 minutes between appointments and ensuring there was a non-negotiable lunch break. He built admin time into his week and committed to logging off at 6pm. He even gave himself permission to decline last-minute bookings, even when it felt tempting to squeeze in 'just one more'.

Ending sessions on time was the hardest habit to break, but once he saw that clients still got value (and sometimes even more clarity from a contained session), he felt liberated. Within weeks, his energy returned, his sessions improved, and he stopped resenting his own business. Time boundaries gave Michael something he hadn't felt in a while, breathing room. He was working less but achieving more and his clients were getting the best version of him.

From Guilt to Growth – Financial Boundaries that Built Stability

Amira loved her clients. She also found it hard to charge full fees, regularly discounted sessions, and had no-show policies she never enforced. She felt guilty for charging 'too much', especially when clients told her they were struggling financially. But behind the scenes, she was struggling too, to pay her rent, to cover business expenses, and to justify staying in private practice.

Through coaching, she began to shift the story. She calculated the real cost of running her business — CPD, admin time, supervision, software, resources. The numbers didn't lie. She wasn't making ends meet, even with a full calendar.

We worked together to reframe her pricing not as a punishment to clients, but as a fair exchange for value and sustainability. She introduced a cancellation policy with compassion and clarity, emailed all her clients to explain the updated fees, and braced herself.

Then she enforced her cancellation policy for the first time. Her client respected it, paid the fee, and rebooked. That moment changed everything. Amira started seeing her pricing not as a barrier, but as a container for quality care. Her boundaries didn't push clients away; they created trust and stability for everyone involved. Now, Amira pays herself a consistent income, invests in her professional development, and feels more confident than ever that she's building a career she can sustain.

The following checklist is designed to help you reflect on the boundaries that might be silently draining your time, energy, and value. Use it as a personal audit and starting point for setting healthier, more sustainable practices.

Which ones are true for you right now? What one boundary will you strengthen this month to protect your time, energy, and value?

Boundary Checkpoint: Are You Breaking Any of These?

- Running over time in sessions without charging or protecting your energy for the next client.
- Answering emails, calls, or DMs after hours, blurring the line between work and personal time.
- Avoiding conversations about money, pricing, or cancellation policies for fear of seeming 'too strict'.

- Writing reports or client resources unpaid, simply because you feel bad charging for 'extra work'.
- Saying yes to every referral or opportunity, even when it does not align with your goals or capacity.
- Taking on clients outside your scope or training because you feel obligated or fear turning someone away.
- Skipping supervision or peer support, believing you do not have time or do not 'need' it right now.
- Using your personal phone or social media for client communication, eroding professional boundaries.
- Sharing too much personal information in sessions, to connect, but ultimately blurring roles.
- Letting client guilt or emotional pressure influence your fees, availability, or service structure.

Which boundaries do you tend to overlook or justify bending? What would change for you and your clients, if you upheld those boundaries more consistently?

Now, I get it, crunching numbers might not be your strength (or your idea of a good time). But if you're the business owner, it's your responsibility to know your numbers and understand your margins. This isn't about becoming an accountant, it's about being informed and intentional. If you're unsure where to start or want reassurance that you're on the right track, seek support from a trusted accountant or bookkeeper. They can walk you through your financial reports and help fine-tune your forecasts so you're not just guessing, you're leading your business with clarity.

Here are three practical actions to help you put this chapter into motion:

1. Calculate the actual cost of running your business (include all categories).
2. Write down three non-negotiable boundaries that will protect your time, energy, and income.
3. Reassess and adjust your pricing to reflect business survival and future growth.

Understanding Funding – Making Medicare and More Work for You

Funding models like Medicare, NDIS, and private insurance can either be a bridge to care or a barrier, and it's up to you, the dietitian, to make them work for your practice and your clients.

Understanding funding models isn't just about compliance or billing, it's about creating access, building sustainable businesses, and delivering the level of care clients truly need. Whether it's Medicare's CCMP or EDMP, NDIS, Workers Compensation, DVA, or private health, each model has unique strengths, limitations, and administrative requirements.

To navigate funding models with confidence, it's essential to understand the key systems you may be working within.

Here's a quick overview of the most common funding streams in private practice dietetics and what they mean for you and your clients:

- Medicare Chronic Conditions Management Plan (CCMP): A referral model that allows clients with chronic conditions to receive subsidised allied health sessions.
- Medicare Eating Disorder Management Plan: A referral model that allows clients with an eating disorder to receive subsidised dietitian and psychology sessions.
- National Disability Insurance Scheme (NDIS): A funding model supporting people with permanent and significant disabilities with individually planned supports.
- Workers Compensation (State Insurance Regulatory Authority: SIRA): A funding model for work-related injuries, requiring collaboration with a support team and a focus on return to work.
- Department of Veterans Affairs (DVA): A government-funded model that allows eligible veterans to receive allied health services with full coverage. Dietitians must be registered providers and follow DVA treatment and reporting guidelines, often supporting clients with chronic disease management, weight maintenance, and recovery post-discharge.
- Private Health Funds: A rebate model where eligible clients can claim part of the cost of dietetic sessions, depending on their extras cover. No GP referral is needed, and dietitians must be registered providers.

UNDERSTANDING FUNDING

When you understand how they work, you can make informed decisions about what to offer, what to decline, and how to advocate for your client beyond the rebate.

Far too often, dietitians in private practice feel pressure to fit into funding systems without question. They bulk-bill Medicare appointments at a loss because 'that's just what you do'. They accept NDIS rates without tracking the admin hours involved or charging for the travel they do. They see clients on referral pathways that don't cover costs and then feel guilty about raising fees or setting boundaries.

But here's the truth: these models are tools, not mandates. You get to decide how, when, and if you use them in your practice. Funding models aren't the boss of your business you are.

Understanding funding gives you freedom. It gives you the freedom to:

- Say yes to referrals that fit your model
- Say no to services that are unsustainable
- Advocate for fair compensation
- Educate your clients and referrers about the true value of your work

It also helps you stay in your lane clinically, ethically, and financially. When you know the requirements and limitations of each model, you're less likely to overpromise, undercharge, or burn out trying to fit yourself into systems that weren't built for your long-term success. Yes, funding models can be confusing. But they can also be empowering when you understand how to work *with* them rather than be controlled *by* them.

This chapter isn't about the rules, these change frequently, so you will need to refer to the associated websites and stay up to date each year. It's about strategy, sustainability, and owning your place as a health professional *and* a business owner.

If you shift your perspective, these models can become powerful tools that increase access, improve care, and support the sustainability of your business. Let's explore some of the most common objections dietitians have about working with funding models, and how to reframe them for clarity, confidence, and impact.

'Medicare only gives me a few sessions. What's the point?'

It's a start, not the whole treatment pathway. Those initial sessions under a Chronic Condition Management Plan (CCMP) are an introduction. They allow you to begin building rapport, educating the client about their condition, and establishing trust. Once that trust is formed, it becomes easier to communicate the value of continued care beyond the rebate. You can begin to frame the CCMP as a gateway, not a destination. Use those initial sessions to deliver quick wins, set achievable goals, and outline what long-term progress might look like, planting the seed early that meaningful change takes time. Oh, and if the referring GP informs the patient that the sessions are 'free', it is absolutely your right to correct this misinformation and charge your actual fee amount.

UNDERSTANDING FUNDING

'It's too complicated to keep track of all the different requirements.'

It can be, but it doesn't have to be. Each funding model does have its own rules, but they're learnable. You don't need to hold it all in your head. Developing templates for your CCMP reports, pre-written NDIS justification paragraphs, and onboarding checklists for each funding type means you're not starting from scratch each time. This reduces admin burden and protects your time. Think of it as building your own internal knowledge bank a playbook that makes compliance simpler, not scarier. Systems and structure turn complexity into clarity.

'Clients won't pay beyond the rebate.'

Some won't. But many will especially when they understand what they're paying for. If all they see is the dollar rebate, then yes, anything more seems expensive. But when you clearly explain what goes into your sessions, your expertise, the planning, the follow-up, the tailored support and extended session time beyond the Medicare time limit they begin to see that your service is far more than a Medicare item number. The rebate becomes a helpful contribution, not the ceiling. Educating clients on the value you provide, reframing the conversation away from 'bulk billing' toward 'high quality healthcare', that's where the shift happens. You're offering more than a transaction; you're delivering a transformation.

When you shift from avoiding funding models to understanding and leveraging them, you unlock a new level of clarity, professionalism, and sustainability in your private practice. It's not just about ticking boxes or securing rebates, it's about using these frameworks to enhance your service delivery, protect your energy, and expand your impact.

Here's what becomes possible when you stop seeing funding as a limitation and start using it as a strategic asset:

Empowers dietitians to choose funding models aligned with their values and business goals
Understanding the differences between funding models gives you the power to make decisions that feel aligned, not just financially, but ethically and professionally. Whether you're passionate about disability support, chronic disease care, or rehabilitation, you get to choose the models that reflect your values and support the way you want to practice. You're no longer at the mercy of what's "popular" or "expected", you can intentionally shape a business that supports the kind of impact you want to make.

Increases client access to care without compromising service quality
When used well, funding pathways can reduce cost barriers for clients, opening doors to dietetic support they might otherwise go without. But access doesn't have to mean burnout. By learning how to structure services, session frequency, and communication within the constraints of funding models and knowing when to step outside them, you can make support accessible *and* sustainable. It's not either/or. This balance protects your energy while helping more people.

Supports compliance with referral and documentation requirements
Templates, systems, and clear procedures help reduce the overwhelm of paperwork and increase your confidence in

being audit-ready. Whether it's a Medicare CCMP report, a NDIS plan review letter, or a SIRA treatment plan, having structured documents in place allows you to stay organised, professional, and in integrity with your obligations. This also helps you build stronger trust with GPs, case managers, and funding bodies because they can count on you for quality communication and transparency.

Encourages sustainable pricing and service delivery
Funding models shouldn't dictate your pricing but understanding how they work allows you to structure fees in a way that supports your long-term business health. Whether you bulk bill, charge a gap, or go fully private, having clarity on what your time, expertise, and admin load are worth gives you confidence to price with purpose. You stop feeling resentful or depleted and start feeling in control of your income, your time, and your clinical boundaries.

Builds trust and transparency with clients and referral networks
Clients and referrers appreciate clarity. When you can confidently explain what a rebate covers (and what it doesn't), how sessions will be structured, and what ongoing support may look like, you immediately stand out as a professional who respects both your client's goals and your own expertise. This strengthens the therapeutic relationship, boosts compliance, and generates word-of-mouth referrals. Transparency builds trust and trust builds thriving practices.

> 'Rebates are the welcome mat, not the entire house.'

In each of the following stories, you'll see how clarity, boundaries, and proactive relationship-building can turn everyday interactions into long-term referral opportunities.

The Informed Referrer

Early in her private practice journey, Sarah, a dietitian, felt unsure about how to stand out when working with GPs. Instead of focusing only on client-facing work, she decided to invest time in developing structured, meaningful CCMP reports and advocating for planned Case Conferences through Medicare funding. She included clinical updates, specific nutrition goals, and clear outcomes and sent them promptly after every appointment. The GPs in her local area took notice. The consistency in her reports plus the encouraging prompt and invitation to collaborate and communicate more closely through case conferences meant that eventually the GP practice got curious, reached out to her to understand more about the case conferencing process, and after some assistance to the GP clinic they started booking 1-2 case conferences.

One GP rang her directly to say, 'Your reports are the only ones I actually read, they help me understand what's going on with my patients'. Plus, in the initial success and benefits of the case conferences meant that they were starting to happen more often and with more GPs from that same clinic. Over the following months, her referrals doubled. She wasn't just using the CCMP for five sessions; she was building professional credibility that extended well beyond it. That connection, built through professionalism and clarity, became a powerful source of consistent referrals even for clients not using rebates at all. Sarah was able to do this sustainably by investing in an AI note-taking system, which streamlined her session notes and GP reports, helping her save time and maintain high quality communication.

The Boundaries Breakthrough

James, a solo dietitian, was approached by a provider offering referrals through an insurance-funded model. The catch? The hourly rate offered was significantly below his breakeven cost. At first, he hesitated, after all, he needed clients. But after reviewing the numbers and reflecting on the workload, he realised that taking those referrals would actually cost him money and drain his time.

Instead of accepting, he respectfully declined and focused on strengthening his private billing systems. He began clearly communicating his pricing structure and offering value-packed service bundles. Referrers and potential clients responded positively, especially when they realised, they were getting consistent support and attention. He attracted more of the right-fit clients who were committed to long-term outcomes. Most importantly, he regained his confidence and protected his financial sustainability. His 'no' created space for even better 'yeses'. It's ok to decline work even if you are not sitting with full calendars, you wouldn't want to fill your time with the wrong clients and payment structures to not be available or focused on the tasks that will bring you aligned clients in the future.

The Confident Communicator

Emily, a paediatric dietitian, began seeing a young child with feeding difficulties whose NDIS funding had been allocated to other therapies. The parents were confused, overwhelmed, and worried about costs. Instead of walking away, Emily offered to help. She provided the family with a letter outlining the functional reasoning for nutrition support, aligned it with the NDIS Practice

Standards, and collaborated with the support coordinator to advocate for a plan review.

Within a few weeks, the child's plan was updated to include dietetic services. Emily then delivered consistent therapy, documented progress, and communicated regularly with the care team. The result? Improved nutritional outcomes for the child, trust and relief from the family, and a strong professional relationship with the coordinator, who now refers other families to Emily's care. Building a strong referral network takes dedicated advocacy for your services and for the clients you want to support. Sitting back and waiting won't bring your ideal clients through the door. You need to be proactive and trust that the help you put into the world will eventually come back around.

These stories aren't just about funding, they're about values, boundaries, and business decisions. When you step into your role with confidence and clarity, you position yourself as a leader in your space, not just a provider of services.

So, let's reframe how you think about funding. Instead of seeing rebates as limitations, what if they became opportunities?

Consider this:

What if you stopped viewing rebates as the finish line of care, and started seeing them as a springboard, an access point that opens the door to deeper, more impactful work with your clients?

What if you felt confident explaining funding models to your clients and referrers, and positioned yourself as a trusted expert?

UNDERSTANDING FUNDING

What if you stopped letting rebates dictate your session structure and pricing?

What if you felt empowered to choose the funding models that best supported your clinical goals *and* your business health?

The more intentional you are with your funding strategy, the more freedom, clarity, and impact you'll create in your private practice. The following three action steps are more than just items on a to-do list; they're levers for change. If you want this chapter to make a real difference in your business, don't just read them, apply them. Reflect, implement, and revisit as needed.

> Action Step 1. Review which funding models align with your services and financial goals.
> Action step 2. Start educating clients that rebates are helpful, but they don't define the full value of your service.
> Action Step 3. Develop clear systems and templates for each model (e.g., CCMP reports, NDIS support letters).

Confident Consultation – Structuring Sessions That Work

Structure creates freedom and reflects credibility. You have the nutrition knowledge, now it's time to strategically support your clients to achieve their health goals through attending more of your sessions.

Many dietitians enter private practice full of nutrition knowledge but unsure how to structure their consultations. They wing it. They over-give. They run out of time. They feel awkward recommending follow-up sessions and get nervous when talking about money.

Here's the truth: structure isn't restrictive, it's empowering.

Clients thrive with structure. They feel safer, clearer, and more willing to commit to change when they understand the process. And as the clinician, structure helps you manage your time, show up with confidence, and deliver consistent results.

But here's the missing link, most dietitians have never been taught *how* private practice sessions should be structured. At university, we learn how to take diet histories, interpret bloods, and apply MNT in a hospital context. We get used to 20-minute reviews or one-off education sessions with patients who may never return. Discharge planning happens quickly, and long-term change is rarely the focus.

In private practice, everything shifts.

You are no longer handing off your client after one touchpoint, you are building a therapeutic relationship that could last months or years. You are leading a health journey that requires trust, communication, and consistent follow-up. And most importantly *you have the opportunity to create lasting change.*

Without structure, many clinicians:

- Fail to gather the right information at the start
- Miss opportunities to reinforce key learnings
- Avoid talking about follow-ups and pricing
- Leave clients feeling unsure about next steps

Structure gives you:

- Professional credibility
- Clear treatment pathways

- Confidence to recommend and rebook
- A better client experience
- Stronger retention and outcomes

When you walk into a session with clarity and purpose, your client senses it. You don't need to script every word, but you *do* need a plan. A framework. A rhythm to how you guide someone through change. You are the leader in the room. When you guide with clarity, clients feel held. When you fumble, they disappear. Structure is what supports you and them.

Before we dive into how to structure impactful consultations, let's get clear on some key terms that will anchor the strategies in this chapter and help you communicate your process with confidence and professionalism.

- Framework: A consistent process you follow to achieve reliable, effective outcomes.
- Assessment appointment: The first 1–3 sessions where you gather information, set goals, and build the roadmap for change.
- Review session/follow-up: Ongoing sessions to implement the plan, overcome barriers, and provide accountability and support.
- Authority: The legitimate power and influence a professional has to make decisions, provide guidance, and direct patient care within their scope of practice.
- Credibility: The degree to which patients and colleagues perceive them as trustworthy, knowledgeable, and competent. It's about earning trust and demonstrating expertise in order to effectively care for patients and build professional relationships.

Even with the best intentions, many dietitians hold back from structuring their sessions or recommending multiple appointments not because they lack the skills, but because they're worried about how it will be perceived. Concerns around sounding 'pushy', not having enough experience, or scaring off clients often get in the way of clear communication and confident care planning. Let's address some of the most common mindset hurdles that can interfere with offering structured, effective support and reframe them with practical, empowering responses.

'I don't want to sound pushy by recommending multiple sessions'

You're not selling a flaky product, you're offering a professional service. Recommending a full treatment plan isn't pushy, it's responsible. You wouldn't expect a physiotherapist to fix chronic pain in one session. Your role is to outline what's required for real change, with compassion and clarity. Mapping out sessions in advance builds trust and sets shared expectations. Clients feel reassured when they know there's a plan in place, and they're more likely to commit when they understand that long-term support is part of the process.

'What if clients don't come back?'

Clients are more likely to return when they understand the process, feel safe and supported, and see the value in your structured approach. It's not about manipulation, it's about making it easy for them to stay engaged and feel successful. When you explain how each session builds on the last, clients feel like they're on a clear and purposeful journey. Returning clients are a reflection of confidence, not pressure.

'But I'm still figuring out my style, I don't want to follow a script'

A structure isn't a script, it's scaffolding. It gives you something solid to lean on while still allowing flexibility and personality. You'll adapt your framework over time as your skills grow. But having something consistent to fall back on helps you stay focused and effective. It creates safety for your clients and efficiency for you. As you gain experience, you'll naturally develop your rhythm within the structure, a signature approach that's recognisably yours.

> *'A confused mind says no.*
> *Clear structure builds confidence.'*

When you have a clear, repeatable process, you can focus less on what to do next and more on delivering meaningful results. Here's what becomes possible when your consultations are designed with clarity and purpose:

Deliver amazing client experiences

When your clients know what to expect, feel heard, and see progress, they talk about it. Happy clients refer others, rebook consistently, and stay committed to the process. Word of mouth marketing is rooted in great service delivery.

Build authority and credibility early

A well-run first session speaks volumes. It communicates that you're organised, thoughtful, and experienced. Clients are more likely to follow your advice and stick with the plan when they trust that you're leading with intention.

Communicate your expertise with confidence

Having a framework means you're not floundering mid-session or getting lost in tangents. You can explain your reasoning clearly, set goals collaboratively, and keep each session productive and purposeful.

Create returning clients who achieve results

The best outcomes come from ongoing care. Structure allows you to recommend appropriate follow-ups without awkwardness. Clients understand the value of coming back because you've made the purpose clear from the start.

Execute effective treatment plans from day one

You gather the right information, build rapport, establish trust, and start making progress immediately. This builds momentum and reinforces your credibility as a skilled clinician.

Assessment Appointment Structure: Making the Most of Every Minute

A well-structured assessment session is the foundation for strong clinical outcomes, confident communication, and efficient time management. Rather than trying to do everything at once, the goal of an initial consultation is to start building trust, gather key information, and set the direction for ongoing support. By being intentional with your time and approach, you can avoid feeling rushed, reduce overwhelm for both you and your client, and lay the groundwork for a high-quality client experience.

Why Structure Matters

The initial consultation is just one part of the assessment process; it's not the whole story. It's your opportunity to build rapport, begin to understand the client's needs, and start co-creating a plan that makes them feel heard, hopeful, and supported.

Many early-career dietitians fall into the trap of thinking they must gather every detail and provide a full intervention in the first session. But rushing through everything can compromise the client's understanding, your clarity, and the overall therapeutic relationship.

Structure gives you a plan. It also helps clients feel confident that they're in good hands. And when your sessions have flow and purpose, you'll deliver better results and feel less exhausted by the end of the day.

Timing Breakdown: A 60-Minute Initial Appointment

Here's a suggested timeline for a 60-minute initial assessment session (50 minutes client-facing + 10 minutes note completion). Having a visible clock in your room can help you stay on track and avoid running over.

Time	Task
0–2 minutes	Welcome the client, invite them into the space, brief check-in
2–5 minutes	Pre-frame the session: clarify structure, purpose, and today's goals
5–20 minutes	Explore client's story: medical history, concerns, lifestyle context
20–35 minutes	Dietary assessment: eating pattern, intake, preferences, rules, routines
35–45 minutes	Goal setting, education, and next steps: co-create the path forward
45–50 minutes	Session wrap-up: summarise, schedule next session, walk client out
50–60 minutes	Complete notes, breathe, reset before the next client

Note: You don't have to gather *every* possible detail about the client in this first session. The goal is to gather what matters most now and plan for what comes next. A comprehensive assessment phase will unfold over multiple sessions. So, take the pressure off yourself and focus on rapport and the client experience just as much as the clinical tasks.

Common pitfalls and mindset reminders:

- You're not behind if you don't deliver an intervention straight away. Rapport-building and clarity of goals are often the most valuable outcomes of session one.
- You don't need to know everything. Get the key pieces today and make a plan to explore the rest over time.
- Personalisation beats perfection. Be curious and collaborative as no two clients are the same.

Practical Assessment Framework (Table)

Use this table to guide the key components to include within your initial consultations to support clinical reasoning, structure note-taking, and keep the session client-centred.

Section	Prompt / What to Cover
Welcome & Rapport Building	Introduce yourself, build rapport, demonstrate curiosity and empathy.
Pre-Framing the Session	Outline the purpose, structure, and what to expect during the session.
Explore Client's Motivation & Goals	Ask why they've come, why now, and explore deeper motivations.
Understand Health Concerns & History	Capture key medical history, symptoms, diagnoses, and treatments.
Comprehensive Diet & Lifestyle Assessment	Include 24-hour recall or diet history, routines, physical activity, stress, sleep.
Review Past Attempts and Challenges	Understand what's been tried before and what has or hasn't worked.
Provide Education & Insight	Offer relevant information, set realistic expectations, normalise common challenges.
Co-Create an Initial Treatment Plan	Agree on 1–3 clear goals, outline barriers, supports, and action steps.
Session Wrap-Up	Recap key points, reflect, plan next session, and final takeaways.

Why Session Length Matters: Time Breakdown and Burnout Prevention

When setting your standard appointment length, it can be tempting to choose shorter sessions in the hope of filling your calendar, reducing fees for clients, or 'keeping things quick'. But here's the reality: shorter sessions often leave too little time to deliver a satisfying session.

Let's compare the available time per key section of an appointment based on a 50-minute vs. 20-minute session:

Session Component	50-min Session	20-min Session
Rapport & Motivation	~12.5 mins	~5 mins
Assessment & History	~12.5 mins	~5 mins
Education & Insight	~12.5 mins	~5 mins
Goal Setting & Wrap-Up	~12.5 mins	~5 mins

In a 20-minute session, you have less than 5 minutes per task, barely enough time to gather information, let alone connect meaningfully, personalise advice, or collaboratively set goals. You may find yourself rushing, skipping important steps, or feeling flustered trying to squeeze too much into too little time.

The result:

- Clients receive less individualised support.
- You leave sessions feeling scattered, not satisfied.
- Burnout creeps in.
- The 'churn-through' model starts to replace quality care.

Short sessions create unsustainable pressure for you and for your clients. They reduce the chance for reflection, empathy, and client buy-in. And when you're constantly up against the clock, your ability to think critically, tailor care, and deliver exceptional service suffers.

By contrast, longer appointments create space. Space for meaningful conversation, shared decision-making, and thoughtful education. Space to understand the person in front of you, not just their food record. When you allow enough time, you'll feel calmer, more confident, and more present. Your sessions become more effective, your client outcomes improve, and your practice becomes something you can actually sustain.

Review Appointment Structure

The review appointment is ideally scheduled for a total of 60 minutes, with 50 minutes dedicated to client interaction and the remaining 10 minutes reserved for note finalisation and a short buffer before the next session. Review sessions offer an essential opportunity to reflect, re-educate, and re-energise your clients.

These appointments are especially beneficial for:

- A client's first review session following assessment
- Clients with more complex presentations
- Clients ready to commit to greater change and wanting to maximise their outcomes
- Dietitians who are building rapport and reinforcing commitment to longer-term care

Offering these longer review appointments allows for a deeper therapeutic relationship and the ability to explore new topics, identify and work through barriers, and enhance the overall effectiveness of treatment.

Timeline Breakdown:

Time	Review Appointments
0–2 minutes	Welcome and bring the client into the room/session
2–5 minutes	Pre-frame session: Set expectations and outline the structure for today
5–20 minutes	Complete any outstanding information from initial assessment: • Finalise/review goals • Review food and symptom diary if provided • What worked well, and why? • What were the challenges, and why?
20–35 minutes	Education on selected topic based on client goals (THE WHAT & WHY)
35–45 minutes	Practical application of education (THE HOW)
45–50 minutes	Pre-frame next session topic based on client goals Book follow-up and walk the client out
50–60 minutes	Finalise notes and allow brief reset before next session

Why Time Matters

To illustrate the difference that session length can make, here's how time breaks down:

Session Component	50-min Session	20-min Session
Rapport + review	~12.5 mins	~5 mins
Solve challenges	~12.5 mins	~5 mins
Education	~12.5 mins	~5 mins
Goal Setting & Wrap-Up	~12.5 mins	~5 mins

Trying to deliver comprehensive, client-centred care in under 30 minutes severely limits your ability to reflect, educate, and individualise your care. It creates pressure for both you and your client, increases cognitive fatigue, and reduces the opportunity for insight, shared decision-making, and behaviour change.

Short sessions are often unsustainable for both the clinician and the client. By offering longer review sessions, especially during the early stages of treatment or with complex cases you protect your energy, honour your clinical reasoning, and deliver a higher standard of care that clients value and return for.

Review Session Essentials:

- Continue to get to know your client: Understand their 'why', their evolving story, and current motivation
- Facilitate reflection: Explore what worked, what didn't, and what barriers may need to be addressed

- Provide continued education: Relate your teaching to their condition, goals, and lived experience
- Refine and recommit to goals: Clarify next steps, co-create action items, and keep momentum going

Don't set yourself up for failure by choosing the shortest time possible. Choose the time that allows you to deliver the care you're proud of. It's better to see fewer clients well than to rush many clients poorly.

> *'Your confidence creates the space*
> *where clients believe change is possible.'*

Now that you've seen how thoughtful session structure enhances time management, builds rapport, and creates a seamless client experience, let's explore how these frameworks come to life in real practice. The following stories illustrate how implementing structured assessment and review templates, clear communication strategies, and confident follow-up planning has transformed both client outcomes and clinician confidence within our team at Optimum Intake.

Assessment Template – Setting the Foundation

When I first introduced a team-wide assessment template, something shifted. Clients started saying, 'This felt so thorough!' Even when individual clinicians had different communication styles, the consistent framework created a predictable and professional experience. It freed up brain space and reduced overwhelm for both the client and the clinician. It also reduced variation in care and allowed us to track client progress more systematically.

This exact assessment template is one of the tools shared in this book. It's the structure we developed at Optimum Intake that had the impact of building confidence in both our new grad team members and those who had been with us for years. Embedding this structure brought a new level of consistency across the team, improved session time efficiency, increased transparency with clients about what the sessions would include (which built trust) and gave dietitians a clear guide for concluding the session and inviting clients back for follow-up care. This has been one of the key tools in significantly increasing our client retention, positive feedback scores, and our team's confidence when running sessions in the private practice setting.

Review Session Structure – Safety and Progress

A client once told me, 'I didn't realise how important the check-ins were until I missed one and felt completely stuck again'. Review sessions aren't just about checking boxes, they're spaces for clients to feel supported, reoriented, and re-motivated. Having a flexible but structured review session template means you're not scrambling to know what to say. It gives each session a clear purpose that aligns with the overall treatment plan.

The review session template included in this book is one of the most appreciated resources by our team. It helps keep you and your client on track, reduces the mental load, and provides consistent touch points for assessing progress and making adjustments. At Optimum Intake, this structure led to better goal setting, more open communication, and gave our clinicians the language to confidently close a session and invite clients to return.

Building Authority and Encouraging Return Clients

It's not about hard-selling the next session. I had a client once say, 'Oh, I thought it was just a one-off session'. That taught me: if we're not communicating the plan, we can't expect clients to commit to the process. When I started openly explaining the expected length of treatment and how we'd tackle it together, not only did rebooking's increase, but clients also started saying, 'I feel like I'm really getting somewhere'. Your authority comes through in how clearly you lead them through the process. Your credibility is reinforced in how consistently you show up.

The session planning templates you'll find in this book mirror the structure we use at Optimum Intake. These tools help you set the tone, outline the journey ahead, and clarify the client's role in that process. Having clear frameworks for treatment timelines, action plans, and even suggested language for rebooking has helped our team of dietitians foster stronger therapeutic relationships, drive better clinical outcomes, and grow their confidence and competence as leaders in their client's health journey.

The Hidden Gap With Our Traditional Training

More often than not, dietetic students graduate without knowing how to plan for the number of sessions a client will likely need to achieve meaningful, lasting change. They're unsure how to map out an approach beyond the first session, or what topics should be covered for each health condition. They haven't been taught how to pace education, weave in mindset coaching, or create space to address a client's real-life barriers.

This lack of structure doesn't just create stress for the clinician — it also impacts client outcomes. Without a clear plan, sessions feel disjointed. Clients don't know what's coming next, they lose momentum, and they don't return. When you end a session without a clear direction for what's coming next, you're missing a key opportunity to keep them engaged, hopeful, and committed to their goals. They should leave feeling like they *can't miss the next session* because they know it's going to be valuable.

Planning your sessions with intention isn't just good clinical practice. It's the key to stronger client retention, better health outcomes, and long-term business sustainability. And ultimately, it's what elevates the reputation of our entire profession. When we practice with structure, we don't just help, we lead.

Mastering Condition-Based Session Planning

Effective session planning in private practice is far more than just knowing what to talk about next, it's a skill that blends clinical reasoning, client-centred care, communication, and business acumen. And it's one of the most underdeveloped skills dietitians bring with them from university into the real world of practice. We're taught how to assess, how to educate, and how to write a nutrition care plan. But we're not taught how to plan a journey, one that unfolds over time, builds momentum, adapts to setbacks, and creates lasting change.

That's where Condition-Based Session Planning comes in.

Why Session Planning Is a Core Skill

Planning out the number of sessions a client is likely to need and what will happen in those sessions isn't just a helpful tool. It's the foundation of trust, confidence, retention, and results.

Poor session planning can leave you (and your client) guessing:

- Are we on track?
- Are they ready to self-manage?
- Have we covered enough?
- Is this still valuable?

On the flip side, structured planning lets you:

- Map out your education and behaviour change strategy
- Keep sessions focused without overwhelming the client
- Clearly communicate expectations and session goals
- Feel confident in how you deliver your service
- Retain clients longer while improving outcomes

But this doesn't mean rigid scripts or 'cookie cutter' plans. The goal is scaffolded individualisation giving yourself a starting framework that allows for tailoring and flexibility as you get to know each client.

What Makes Session Planning Complex?

There are multiple layers to get right and learning to master each takes time and practice. Here's why this skillset deserves your attention and intention:

Condition Complexity

The number of sessions needed will vary based on what you're treating. A client with PCOS, IBS, or disordered eating will need a very different care pathway to someone who just needs help reading food labels.

Session planning involves knowing how many sessions are likely needed for different conditions and how to sequence those sessions to create progress, not just information dumps.

Client Readiness and Individual Capacity

Even clients with similar diagnoses will have different goals, life circumstances, and motivation levels. A well-structured plan takes into account:

- Where the client is starting from
- Their ability to engage with and apply information
- Their support systems and readiness for change

This means every plan needs both clinical direction and emotional attunement.

Balancing Education and Counselling

Private practice isn't just about providing nutrition education. It's about guiding change and that includes:

- Listening to values and barriers

- Identifying resistance or ambivalence
- Co-creating goals and actions

A great plan combines what, why, and how: what needs to change, why it matters, and how the client will actually do it.

Time Constraints and Session Pacing

Trying to teach everything in one session? It's a fast track to client overwhelm and poor retention. Learning to pace your education over multiple sessions is one of the most powerful tools you can develop. It lets your clients:

- Build skills step-by-step
- Feel successful early
- Stay engaged and curious
- Return for follow-up care

Trying to overdeliver in one session not only dilutes the impact it shortchanges your business and your client.

Where the Value Is Added

You may worry that creating these session frameworks is too 'generic'. But in reality, this is where much of your value lies. Clients don't know how many sessions they need, and they certainly don't know the order of topics that will help them succeed. That's your job. Providing this structure makes you a leader in their health journey, not just someone who answers questions.

More importantly, structured planning helps clients stay on track and complete the work. When clients leave with clarity about what's coming next and why it matters, they're far more likely to return, follow through, and succeed.

And when clients succeed, they refer others. Your reputation grows. Your impact grows. Your income becomes more consistent.

Condition-Based Frameworks: The 'Secret Weapon' for Dietitians

Condition-Based Session Planning Frameworks offer a scaffold to start with not a script to follow. At Optimum Intake, we've developed these frameworks for many of the most common clinical areas, and they've transformed the way our team communicates, educates, and plans treatment.

Whether you're supporting someone with PCOS, IBS, disordered eating, or bariatric surgery recovery, having a mapped-out plan allows you to:

- Explain the purpose of ongoing care
- Set realistic expectations early
- Guide clients through a stepwise process
- Reduce drop-off and churn
- Feel more confident in your clinical impact

Your Next Step

Start creating your condition-based guides. You can start by using and adapting the below template to help you build your own Condition-Based Session Planning Frameworks. Start with just one condition, perhaps the one you most commonly see, or the one you want to specialise in.

Remember: you're not locking yourself into a rigid plan. You're giving yourself a map so you can guide clients more confidently, and show them that nutrition change is not a one-time conversation, it's a process worth investing in.

Example: PCOS – Condition-Based Session Planning Framework

To help bring this concept to life, here's a complete example of how to structure a condition-specific care plan for clients with Polycystic Ovary Syndrome (PCOS). This framework supports both the client's experience and the clinician's confidence ensuring sessions are purposeful, progressive, and personalised.

Session	Focus Area	Client Activities / Homework	Resources Needed
1	Assessment, goal setting, PCOS education	Complete food & symptom diary	Client goal sheet, PCOS overview
2	Nutrition planning, insulin resistance	Trial new meal structure, track hunger cues	Meal planning handout, hunger guide
3	Movement, mindset, stress management	Identify enjoyable movement, reflect on body image beliefs	Activity menu, journal prompts
4	Supplement review and troubleshooting	Trial recommended protocol	Supplement safety handout
5	Lifestyle barriers and strategy support	Identify habits to adjust, create environment plan	Customised strategy summary
6	Confidence & sustainability	Create long-term maintenance plan	Success reflection worksheet

How to Explain This Plan to Clients

Here is what I would say: 'To help you reach your goals, we'll work together over several sessions. I've mapped out a plan based on what we have covered in your assessment, and we'll take it step by step. Each session has a focus, and we'll build on your progress together. Most clients benefit from 5 to 8 sessions to really make meaningful and lasting change.'

Having this conversation early helps manage expectations, normalise follow-up, and reframe the service as a process, not a one-off consult. The plan is flexible can be amended as more or less support may be needed and this is where the individualisation begins. Start with the framework and adjust to the client.

This framework is just one example. The more you practice this style of planning, the more intuitive it will feel and the more confident you'll be guiding clients toward real, sustainable transformation.

Without these skills, you'll churn and burn through clients. You'll feel unfulfilled, unsure of your impact, and financially insecure. You'll constantly be trying to get new clients to fill your calendar instead of keeping the ones you have. Confidence grows when structure supports your sessions.

What if a client declines the full number of sessions you recommend?

That's completely okay. Your responsibility is to outline the optimal treatment pathway, not to control whether the client follows it.

When you've clearly communicated what's required for real, lasting change, you've done your job. From there, the client is making an informed decision based on their current circumstances whether it's time, finances, or simply a desire to 'try things out' before committing further.

If a client feels hesitant to book all sessions upfront, you can meet them where they're at. Start with the number of sessions they feel most comfortable with. Reframe the plan to suit that shorter timeline, not by trying to squeeze everything in, but by choosing which areas to prioritise and which will need to wait.

Then, when those initial sessions are complete, check in. Ask if they'd like to continue with the full plan or pause for now. Always leave the door open. Your role is to support, not pressure. Often, once trust is built and clients experience the value of your care, they become more open to continuing. By maintaining clarity, flexibility, and professionalism, you're reinforcing both your credibility and your client's autonomy and that's what long-term therapeutic relationships are built on.

Let's turn this knowledge into action.

It's not enough to simply understand the importance of structure, confidence, and session planning. Implementation is where transformation happens.

Whether you're just starting out or refining your existing practice, these three actions will help you solidify your value, enhance client outcomes, and build a more sustainable, results-driven business.

1. Use a framework for your sessions, create your own flavour and be known for it.
2. Plan how many sessions on average your clients need to gain the full outcomes of their goals with you and offer that as a minimum. Anything less is doing a disservice.
3. Track your clients' lifetime value, how many sessions are your clients receiving from you before achieving their goals? How many of your clients reach full program completion? Increase your percentage toward 100%.

From Advice to Action – Planning Treatment That Delivers Results

Too often, clients leave a nutrition consult with advice, but no clear plan, and that's where their progress stalls.

What if every client left your consult feeling clear, hopeful, and ready to take action because you gave them not just advice, but a written roadmap? And I'm not referring to a sheet of paper where you have scribbled down several recommendations in your messy handwriting, hoping that they can read it.

Many early-career dietitians hesitate to create a formal treatment plan document, thinking it might be too rigid, too clinical, or too time-consuming. Sometimes there's a fear it will overwhelm the client. Other times, it's self-doubt: 'I don't feel confident in what the plan should be.'

But here's the truth: treatment plans are one of the most powerful tools we have for improving outcomes, increasing accountability, and deepening connection.

Clients come to us in a state of uncertainty. They've often tried and failed on their own. They're tired of being told what to do without a clear sense of how to do it. A treatment plan gives shape to the conversation. It reinforces the value of the session and says: *'I heard you. I see where you want to go. Here's how we'll start.'*

A clear, collaborative plan:

- Gives structure to what was discussed, so it doesn't just disappear into memory
- Clarifies the next steps, reducing anxiety and guesswork between sessions
- Shows the client that you respect their time, effort, and decision to seek help

This is especially important in private practice, where retention and outcomes rely heavily on trust, communication, and perceived value. If a client walks out with just vague advice or too many suggestions, they may feel unsure and not come back. But when they leave with a written plan tailored to their goals, it builds momentum.

And this isn't about perfection. You don't need the 'perfect' treatment plan. You need a working plan, one that evolves as your client learns, struggles, and grows. You're not handing them a rigid checklist. You're inviting them into a partnership, saying: *'Let's do this together.'*

If you're still early in your career, don't wait to feel ready. Start small. Focus on clarity, not complexity. Even a few bullet points can make a world of difference.

Clients forget up to 80% of what's said in a session. Let's make sure the important parts stick and treatment plans are how we do that.

The following terms are essential to developing a structured, collaborative approach to care, helping you communicate your value, build trust, and ensure clients feel supported every step of the way. Let's define them clearly so you can begin to apply them with purpose.

1. Treatment Plan: A collaborative, written summary that outlines what was discussed, the client's key motivators, and the agreed-upon next steps.
2. 'Why Now': The tipping point or emotional driver that led the client to seek support at this time.

To help you put these concepts into practice, here's a sample treatment plan template. This structure is designed to clearly capture the key elements of your sessions, making it easier to reflect, plan, and communicate next steps with your clients. Use it as a starting point and adapt it to suit your style, client needs, and clinical focus.

Nutrition Treatment Plan

Date: _____

Client Name: _____

Clinician: _____

Presenting conditions or problem: _____

Future impact if left unaddressed: _____

Timeline to feel better: _____

Why is it important to resolve / improve this, now?: _____
_____

Why you're ready to make a change now: _____
_____

Client Goals:

1. _____

2. _____

3. _____

Action Steps (from today's appointment):

1. _____

2. _____

Recommended Treatment Session Frequency:

_____

You might be thinking, 'But what if...?' That's totally normal. A few common concerns tend to pop up when dietitians start using written treatment plans. Let's walk through them and reframe those doubts into something that works for you *and* your clients.

I don't want to overwhelm the client with too much detail

A written plan actually reduces overwhelm. Clients feel reassured knowing their next steps are mapped out. When you take time to distil the session into 2–4 actionable steps, it gives clients a sense of direction, not confusion. It helps them focus their energy on what matters most and helps them feel like the plan is manageable. Clients feel less pressure to 'remember everything' and more confident in taking that first step.

What if the client doesn't follow the plan?

The plan is a living document; it evolves with the client. The act of creating it together builds trust and buy-in. Even if clients don't follow every step, the process of having a plan gives you both a foundation to reflect on what's working and what needs adjusting. You can use their feedback to modify the next steps, identify hidden barriers, and work collaboratively, which is often more powerful than rigid adherence to a plan.

Can't I just have generic plans for each health condition and give that to my clients?

While templates are a great starting point, truly effective treatment plans are personalised. A generic handout doesn't reflect the client's unique goals, challenges, or motivations. Clients are more likely to commit to a plan they co-created with you, one that honours their individual needs and feels doable in their real life. Templates should guide your thinking, not replace your connection. Personalisation is what turns your advice into meaningful action.

> *'A treatment plan turns a conversation into a commitment.'*

To show you what this can look like in real life, here are three moments from my own practice where a clear, collaborative treatment plan made all the difference, for the client, and for the dietitian.

The Client Who Felt Seen

Jasmine was a new client, hesitant and unsure if nutrition support would help. She'd seen other health professionals before and felt like just another name on their schedule. But at the end of her first session, she received a personalised treatment plan that summarised her concerns, reflected her values, and mapped out three achievable goals. It included her 'why now', her personal goals, and a rough outline of what each follow-up would involve. Jasmine told her dietitian, 'This is the first time I've felt really heard.' That treatment plan became a touchstone, something she referred back to when doubt crept in. She even took the treatment plan to her next GP appointment to show her doctor what had been discussed and planned with the dietitian. And now, she keeps a copy of it on her refrigerator. For Jasmine, the plan made her feel seen, capable, and genuinely hopeful.

The Team Breakthrough

When the treatment plan process was first introduced across our team, not everyone was excited. Some saw it as just another task to squeeze into an already packed assessment appointment. Others worried it would add to their workload, or felt unsure about what to write. But what quickly became apparent was the shift it created both in clinician confidence and in client outcomes. It stretched our consultation and questioning skills, pushing us to understand each client's deeper 'why now' motivator, rather than settling for surface-level goals like 'I want to eat healthier'. We began mapping out the number of sessions to recommend at that very first appointment, a new habit that required a shift in how we communicated our support process. Each team member had to reflect on what tools, strategies, and topic areas they'd use to support change, and when and how to check in on progress. Once implemented, the benefits were undeniable: clients felt seen, supported, and committed. Retention and engagement soared. And perhaps most importantly, our team developed greater confidence in recommending and inviting return visits, knowing exactly what they'd be covering next. The treatment plan became a shared language across our team, used in every new assessment, with consistent results.

The Clarity Creator

Sophie, the mother of a 6-year-old child with ARFID, was overwhelmed. She didn't know what to expect from dietetic support and felt paralysed by conflicting advice. She had already spent many months seeing other feeding therapists and had seen very little improvement in her daughter's eating. Sophie was desperate, especially given her daughter's faltering growth, the teasing she was experiencing at school, and the difficult conversations Sophie had to have with her teachers about the lack of fruit and vegetables in her lunchbox. They just didn't understand. After their initial appointment, the dietitian sent a child-friendly, step-by-step treatment plan that explained what they'd focus on, what not to worry about yet, and how they'd measure progress. One of the key steps was for the dietitian to produce a letter to the school, explaining Sophie's strategy and 'approving' what was in her daughter's lunchbox as exactly what was needed right now. A diet analysis was also included in the treatment plan. Although Sophie was initially embarrassed to share the limited food range, the analysis highlighted the nutrients her daughter was getting, guided how to meet her energy needs, and helped them plan what to introduce next. It also identified a key social goal, helping her daughter eat family meals and participate in social eating at places like the local bowling club or friend's houses. That single document eased Sophie's anxiety, empowered her parenting, and improved the family's ability to follow through between sessions. The action plan gave her clarity, direction, and a sense of partnership.

When you take the time to create a personalised treatment plan with your client, you're not just organising the session, you're setting the stage for better outcomes, stronger relationships, and a more confident experience for both of you.

Here's why this matters:

Provides clarity and focus for clients
When clients leave your session with a clear, personalised plan of action, they're no longer guessing what to do next. This clarity helps them stay focused between sessions and reduces the stress of trying to remember everything discussed. It creates an anchor, something they can revisit when things feel overwhelming. It's one of the simplest yet most powerful ways to support follow-through and reduce dropout.

Strengthens motivation by capturing the client's 'why now'
Your client's initial motivation is often deeply emotional, a tipping point that led them to finally seek support. By capturing that 'why now' in writing, you're helping them hold onto that spark when motivation inevitably dips. It also allows you to revisit their original reason when they hit challenges, helping them reconnect to what matters most and stay engaged with the process

Offers a clear reference point for progress and reflection
With a treatment plan, both you and the client have a documented roadmap to refer back to. This makes it easier to track progress, celebrate wins, and make informed adjustments over time. Instead of vague check-ins 'How did you go this week?' you can have meaningful conversations about what worked, what didn't, and what needs tweaking. It turns your sessions into purposeful progress reviews.

Enhances the perceived value of your service
In private practice, the client experience is everything. A thoughtful, well-structured treatment plan shows clients that you've listened, you care, and you have a clear strategy for helping them move

forward. It reinforces your professionalism and makes your service feel more comprehensive. When clients see the value, they're more likely to rebook, refer others, and feel confident they've invested in the right support.

> To wrap up this chapter, here are three practical actions you can take right away to start building stronger, more collaborative treatment plans that support client progress and boost your confidence in session delivery.
>
> 1. End every initial consultation with a written treatment plan (use an AI notetaking tool for efficiency).
> 2. Capture the client's 'why now' and use it as a foundation for treatment.
> 3. Use the treatment plan as a collaborative tool, not a checklist.

Reporting With Impact – Writing Reports That Matter

Report writing doesn't just tick a box, it tells the story of your client's progress, advocates for their needs, and strengthens your professional credibility.

In private practice, many dietitians avoid or under-deliver on report writing, either because they're not paid for it, they don't know what to include, or they feel it's not valued.

But in reality, report writing is one of the most effective ways we can:

- Communicating our clinical reasoning
- Demonstrating value to referrers and support teams
- Improving client access to funding and services
- Enhancing continuity of care

A strong report reflects your thinking, your professionalism, and your commitment to client outcomes. It's how we translate our one-on-one work into system-wide impact.

The problem? Most dietitians were never taught how to write reports in a meaningful, efficient, and outcome-focused way, especially not for private practice settings. And as a result, report writing becomes a rushed task, something left until the last minute or a task that you agonise over every word wondering if this is enough, or clinically correct, wasting too much time on something that you may not be getting paid to do.

When you shift your mindset to see reporting as a service in itself, one that contributes to funding decisions, interprofessional care, and client empowerment, everything changes.

You stop viewing reports as a burden. You start seeing them as a bridge.

That's why I created the Report Writing Wheel, a visual guide to help you determine the purpose for a report, what elements to find value in to help motivate you when you are snowed under with a backlog of what feels like a burden of reports to catch up on.

Knowing the purpose for each report and giving it greater meaning, rather than viewing it as 'just another report to tick off', plus helping you to reprioritise what needs to be in the reports, how much detail to include, whether there is financial payment involved, and how much time needs to be set aside will help you see that not all reports are created equal. You can be smart and efficient with your report writing requirements.

Imagine an old wooden spoke wheel that has 8 sections. Each section on The Report Writing Wheel highlights different considerations to your report writing efficiency:

1. Advocacy – Is this report helping the client secure additional supports or services?
2. Education – Are you explaining nutrition care or interventions to other professionals?
3. Informing – Is this an update or progress report for the GP, specialist, or care team?
4. Promotions – Does this report subtly position you as an expert or trusted provider (building referral networks)?
5. Team Communication – Is this report keeping the multidisciplinary team on the same page?
6. Time Investment – How much time is required to complete this report? Is your time being compensated?
7. Requirements – What funding or compliance boxes need to be ticked (NDIS, DVA, Medicare)?
8. Financial Compensation – Does your current pricing structure cover this report writing? If not, how will you adjust it?

This framework supports you to:

- Determine the purpose for your report
- Consider who will have access and read this report
- Set a time limit for your report writing
- Decide what needs to be included in your report template
- Decide whether you will charge for this report as a separate item

Connecting with the bigger picture of why we use reports, seeing the broader potential impact of your report, along with time-saving templates, checklists, and pricing strategies, you'll not only become a better communicator you'll be a more sustainable practitioner, too.

Now that you've seen how the many elements are considered when planning a report writing task, let's tackle some of the common concerns dietitians have about putting it into practice and how to overcome them.

No one reads the reports anyway

It might feel that way sometimes, but many GPs, support coordinators, and case managers absolutely do read your reports, especially when they're clear, relevant, and easy to understand. In fact, quality reports often become the reason you're trusted with more referrals.

It takes too long and I'm not getting paid for it

That's a pricing and process issue, not a reason to skip the report. You can build report writing time into your service fees or bill for it separately. Establishing a report template that has prefilled sections that you can edit, or using an AI notetaking app can help take the heavy lifting from your reporting tasks. The Report Writing Wheel helps you write efficiently, saving time and energy.

I feel bad spending more time on one type of report and not on others, I have a mix of brief reports and complex ones. Is that okay?

Not all reports are created equal, and they don't need to be. Some reports will require more detail, collaboration, and time than others. That's why using a framework like the Report Writing Wheel helps you assess the purpose, time investment, and value of each report. This ensures you allocate your effort appropriately without guilt and get smarter about your reporting process overall.

How to Price for Report Writing

One of the most common reasons dietitians dislike report writing is that they feel like they're not getting paid properly for it!

Here's how to fix that:

- Identify the true time investment.
    - Track how long you actually spend on each type of report, including review of notes, writing, proofreading, and admin.
    - Many dietitians underestimate this and undercharge as a result.
- Include writing time in your service fees.
    - If the report is *required* as part of your clinical service (e.g., Medicare care plans, NDIS), ensure your session fee covers both direct consultation time and the writing time.
    - Example: If a consult takes 60 mins and the required report takes 20 mins, price your service accordingly either as an 80 min service or using an add-on fee.
- Use separate fees for optional or complex reports.

- For detailed insurance reports or advocacy letters, charge an additional report writing fee, with clear communication to the client and/or funder.
- Example: "Insurance Progress Report — $180 per report (based on 45 mins writing time)"
• Create a menu of report types & fees.
    - List common reports your practice provides and set standard pricing, this makes it easy to communicate with clients and referrers and ensures consistency.
• Review and update regularly.
    - As your efficiency and experience improves, adjust your templates and pricing you should be fairly compensated for the value your report delivers.

Reminder

Time spent writing reports is *billable clinical time*. Your expertise and written communication add enormous value, never give this away for free.

Here are some examples of how being purposeful, strategic and valuing report writing in your business can help it grow.

Improves communication with referral sources and funders
A well-structured report isn't just paperwork, it's a professional handshake. It introduces you to other providers, summarises your expertise, and shows you're paying close attention to your client's needs. Clear reports help build trust with GPs, specialists, support coordinators, and funders, making collaboration smoother and more respectful. And when you consistently deliver high-quality reports, your name stays top of mind for referrals.

Supports client access to ongoing funding and services
Your words can change someone's access to care. An evidence-based, clearly written report that links nutrition to function and outcomes can be the difference between a client receiving 10 hours of support or none at all. Reports written with confidence and intention help ensure your clients continue to receive the services they need to thrive, not just survive.

Strengthens professional identity and recognition
In a crowded and competitive healthcare sector, how you communicate your work matters. Thoughtful, structured reports show that you're not just a practitioner, you're a clinician with a voice, insights, and impact. Reports done well position dietitians as essential, not optional. They elevate the visibility of our profession and remind the system that we're here to create real, measurable change.

Saves time and reduces overwhelm with structured templates
Most dietitians don't struggle with report writing because they lack knowledge, they struggle because they lack clarity. The Report Writing Wheel doesn't tell you exactly what to include in a report, but it gives you a decision-making tool to guide your thinking. It helps you identify the purpose of each report, encourages you to determine how much time and detail is needed, and decide whether financial compensation is appropriate. This mental framework reduces the guesswork and cognitive load, helping you write more efficiently, feel less overwhelmed, and produce work that feels purposeful, not just obligatory.

Adds value to your services and justifies pricing
Clients aren't just paying for a conversation, they're paying for outcomes, clarity, and coordinated care. When your reports

communicate progress, goals, and advocacy, they become a visible and tangible extension of your service. This justifies your fees, supports your pricing model, and allows you to do your best work without feeling like you're giving away hours for free. Charging for reports doesn't make you greedy, it makes your practice sustainable.

> 'A report is more than a summary; it's a voice for your client when you're not in the room.'

Now that we've covered why reports matter, let's look at how you can make them work for

you, along with some real-world examples that show these strategies in action

The GP Who Called to Say Thank You

Emma, a dietitian working in a mixed-billing clinic, used to dash off quick, vague reports just to meet the referral requirements. One day her client who was having a difficult time getting her doctor to understand the non-diet approach, asked if she could please write to the GP to help communicate the approach they were using and highlight aspects of the GP appointments that felt unaligned to this approach and what language felt hurtful to the client. So, Emma agreed to write to the GP. She felt emotionally motivated with the purpose to better inform the GP of all the good work and progress they were making and shared her concern that some conflicting information could jeopardise long-term outcomes.

Emma included references to research articles and encouraged the GP to arrange a case conference under Medicare if they would like to discuss it further. One day, the GP called her. Although it wasn't a planned case conference meeting, the GP thanked Emma and said, 'This is one of the best dietitians reports I've read, thank you for making it so insightful.' That call led to a steady stream of referrals from that practice. Her reports weren't just a compliance task anymore; they became a professional asset that can lead to positive change.

The Confidence Shift with NDIS

Jess worked with several clients under NDIS but always felt unsure whether her reports were 'good enough', despite attending multiple dietitian-specific disability report writing webinars, workshops, and using recommended templates. With coaching, we looked deeper into her report writing worries and found that she highly valued communication, transparency, and wanted her reports to advocate sufficiently for her participants.

This identification and connection to her values, along with using the Report Writing Wheel, allowed for a conversation and reflection on the sustainability of her emotional energy and time spent on report writing and the bigger impact this was having in her business. She was ticking all the report essentials and making them highly personalised, but at the cost of excessive time and not adequately charging for it.

Jess made some template tweaks to standardise some sections of the report, developed a more balanced view of report writing when taking into account all the components of the Report Writing

Wheel, and was able to reduce her report writing time. She felt confident to charge for the time used to produce the report and maintained her high-quality output while sustaining her success rate of receiving full funding amounts for her clients when she did her yearly self-reporting evaluation.

The Pricing Pivot

One approach we used to increase our overall billable utilisation rates across the team was to look into what was taking up our clinicians' time when not with clients doing direct billable tasks. This highlighted how often we were being asked to write a report or create a letter of support and doing so by cramming the task in between client sessions. The reports and letters felt rushed, not created to the high standards that felt aligned to our values and other work we produced and honestly, sometimes a bit of a waste, because what sounded like an urgent request from a client, led to a document that may or may not have been written in time for use with its intended purpose. It wasn't anything we felt proud of.

So, our solution was to support our team to value their contribution and clinical expertise that goes into reports and make them a billable item, one that, if the client wanted it completed, would be paid for upfront and then given an appointment time in the calendar. This ensured we had a date and time of when it would be completed and sent back to the client. It also screened out those who didn't really need a letter or report, as they didn't want to pay or invest in our clinicians producing it.

When we first introduced paid reporting options into our private practice, some team members were hesitant. Would clients think we were being greedy? Would referrers be put off? But what we found was the opposite. When clients understood that the report was part of a comprehensive service, they valued it more. Referrers appreciated the professionalism. And our team stopped feeling burnt out by after-hours administration. The simple act of pricing for reporting created space for quality, confidence, and care.

What if report writing wasn't something you dreaded but something that actually amplified your impact and connected your work to a wider network of care?

> Use these reflection prompts to help you evaluate your approach to report writing, then decide if you need to make some adjustments based on the Report Writing Wheel.
>
> 1. Are there any reports where I'm spending more time than is financially viable?
> 2. Are there reports where I could improve my advocacy or promotional impact?
> 3. Which reports need better templates to save me time?
> 4. Where do I need to update my fees or service agreement to reflect report writing time?
> 5. How could I better communicate my value through my reports?

Getting the Job – Private Practice Interview Secrets

Getting your dream job in private practice isn't just about having the right qualifications, it's about being strategic, intentional, and authentic in your application and interview.

Private practice is one of the fastest-growing areas for dietitians, yet it's also one of the most misunderstood when it comes to getting hired. Unlike hospitals or public health settings, private practices are small businesses. That means hiring decisions are made differently, priorities are different, and what makes someone a *great* candidate isn't always what you were taught to focus on at university.

Why is this important?

Because many dietitians miss out on incredible roles, not because they aren't capable, but because they don't know how to show up with the right insight, preparation, or self-awareness.

- Some dietitians apply broadly, saying yes to any role out of fear of missing out, rather than taking the time to understand whether the role and the company align with their values, goals, or current needs.
- Others don't understand what private practice employers are looking for. (Hint: it's not a perfect GPA or your ability to quote nutrition guidelines, it's your warmth, initiative, curiosity, and ability to communicate.)
- Most applicants submit the same generic cover letter to every job and wonder why they never get a call back.

Private practice roles are often deeply relational, between you and your clients, and between you and the team. That means employers are hiring not just for *skills*, but for *fit*. They want to know:

- Will you add value to the culture?
- Are you coachable and open to feedback?
- Will you help the business grow, or drain its resources?

This chapter matters because it equips you to interview with clarity, confidence, and intention. You'll stop guessing what employers want and start showing them exactly what makes *you* worth hiring.

Here are three terms that you may hear regularly talked about during an interview:

1. Company Culture: The values, beliefs, and behaviours that shape a team's day-to-day experience. It's how "things are done" beyond policies and handbooks.
2. Transferable Skills: Non-clinical skills like communication, time management, emotional intelligence, and problem-solving that apply across roles and industries.
3. Professional Fit: The degree to which your goals, personality, and working style align with the workplace's needs and environment.

Successful interviewing isn't about being the most experienced candidate. It's about being the most *aligned*, *self-aware*, and *prepared*. And when you do that, you don't just get a job. You step into a role that supports your career, your growth, and your confidence as a private practice dietitian.

Interviews can stir up all sorts of nerves and not always for the reasons you think. Sometimes it's not your skills that trip you up, but the stories you tell yourself before you even walk into the room. These thoughts can chip away at your confidence, making you feel like you need to shrink or settle, even when you're more than capable.

Let's break down a few of these and reframe them so they stop holding you back.

I'm just grateful to be considered, I can't be picky

Gratitude is important, but so is discernment. You are not a burden for having standards and values. You're allowed to seek a role that feels supportive, energising, and aligned with your goals, even as a new grad. Being selective doesn't mean you're arrogant or entitled; it means you care about your long-term sustainability and success. If you accept a role out of desperation, chances are you'll be looking again within a few months, burnt out, disillusioned, or stuck. Taking time to assess fit and alignment now saves you (and the employer) a lot of unnecessary turnover later.

I don't have enough experience to stand out

Experience isn't just about how many jobs you've had — it's about the way you show up. Think broadly: have you supported a friend through a tough health journey? Led a group project at university? Worked retail or hospitality? All those experiences shape how you connect with clients, handle pressure, and communicate professionally. In private practice, emotional intelligence, initiative, and a learning mindset often matter more than years on the job. Don't downplay the value of who you are and what you bring beyond the textbook.

The interview is just about technical questions

Maybe in a hospital panel interview, but not in private practice. Most private practice interviews are relational, often 1:1, and more like a conversation than a test. Employers want to see who you are, not just what you know. They're asking themselves: Will my clients feel safe with you? Will you respond well to feedback? Will you bring energy, curiosity, and care to the team? Your ability to hold a natural, honest conversation, not just recite guidelines, is often what seals the deal. Being prepared, but human, is your greatest strength.

> *'Don't choose a job for the money,
> choose it for the mentor'* – Simon Sinek

When you prepare for interviews and job applications with the right mindset, you're not just ticking boxes, you're setting yourself up for a career that actually feels good to be in. The way you approach these early opportunities can shape everything from your day-to-day satisfaction to your long-term growth in private practice. Let's break down the key benefits you'll experience when you bring clarity, confidence, and intention to the process.

You'll find a workplace where you feel supported and aligned

When you approach job applications and interviews with clarity, intention, and self-awareness, you're far more likely to land somewhere that genuinely *feels right*. Instead of accepting the first offer out of fear, you'll know what kind of environment brings out your best, whether it's a team that values mentorship, a business with clear systems, or a clinic aligned with your approach to client care. Alignment reduces burnout and increases job satisfaction, and that makes all the difference in the early years of private practice.

You'll be able to articulate your strengths clearly and authentically

When you understand what makes you valuable, even without years of experience, you can communicate it in a way that feels honest and grounded. You'll be able to say, 'Here's how I approach challenges,' or 'This is the feedback I've received from mentors,' or 'This is what energises me about dietetics.' That kind of clarity stands out. Private practice employers want to hire *people*, not resumes. Your self-awareness and ability to tell your story well are what build connection and credibility.

You'll leave interviews feeling confident, regardless of the outcome

Interviewing with the right mindset, not to *impress*, but to *connect and explore*, helps shift the power dynamic. You'll no longer feel like you're waiting to be chosen. Instead, you'll feel proud of how you showed up, asked questions, and engaged in meaningful conversation. Even if you don't get the job, you'll walk away knowing it was a step forward in your growth and a valuable learning experience for the next opportunity. Confidence doesn't come from getting everything perfect, it comes from showing up with preparation, curiosity, and integrity.

You'll know how to assess whether a company is a fit for you

Instead of asking, 'Will they like me?' you'll start asking, 'Do I like them?' This subtle shift changes everything. You'll learn how to read between the lines, from how they communicate their values, to the questions they ask, to the energy of the interview itself. Do they prioritise mentoring? Are they clear about expectations? Do they speak respectfully about clients and team members? These insights help you evaluate not just the *role*, but the *environment* so you can make decisions that support your wellbeing and career path.

GETTING THE JOB – PRIVATE PRACTICE INTERVIEW SECRETS

You'll feel empowered to craft a career, not just take a job

Private practice can be more than just a place to work. It can be the launchpad for a long, meaningful, and flexible career. By approaching your job search with this long-term view, you'll start thinking about what you want to learn, how you want to grow, and who you want to learn from. You'll feel empowered to shape your career intentionally, rather than drifting from job to job hoping one feels right. This chapter helps you move from passive job seeker to proactive professional, one who chooses with purpose and builds with confidence.

It's one thing to talk about showing up with clarity and confidence, it's another to see how it plays out in real life. These stories bring the concepts in this chapter to life, showing how preparation, alignment, and the right mindset can completely change the way an interview feels and the opportunities it creates.

Whether it's bouncing back from a setback, demonstrating deep values alignment, or asking the kind of questions that leave a lasting impression, these examples show what's possible when you approach interviews with purpose.

From Placement to Practice

Amy was fresh out of university when she first applied for a role at Optimum Intake. She had done her research she knew the clinic's values, had read through the website thoroughly, and even brought up examples from her aged care placement to demonstrate her initiative and interpersonal strengths. But despite her preparation, nerves got the better of her during the interview.

She struggled to clearly articulate her ideas and hesitated when asked about how she might handle certain client scenarios. While her warmth and passion came through, it was clear she lacked confidence in her communication, something that's essential in a private practice setting. After the interview, the hiring team made the difficult decision not to offer her the position. But they could see her potential.

Amy took the feedback to heart, not as a rejection, but as a redirection. Over the next eight months, she took on several short-term contracts and casual roles in community and residential aged care, using each experience to develop her clinical and communication skills. She sought out feedback, attended supervision, and gradually found her voice.

When a new position opened at Optimum Intake, Amy applied again. This time, the difference was clear. She showed up with confidence, communicated her ideas with clarity, and demonstrated greater insight into how she worked in a team. Her ability to connect with others had grown and so had her belief in herself.

She was offered the position, which aligned even more closely with her strengths than the original role. With support, mentoring, and a values-aligned team behind her, Amy has since thrived. Her story is a reminder: a 'no' doesn't mean 'never', it can simply mean 'not yet'. And with time, reflection, and growth, the right opportunity often circles back around when you're truly ready to rise into it.

Aligning With the Vision

Melissa was applying for a paediatric dietitian role with Optimum Intake. Although she had limited direct experience in private practice, she took time to research the company deeply. She read the website thoroughly, reviewed the clinic's paediatric service pages, explored their Instagram content @child.family.nutritionist, and reflected on the language used in their blog posts and mission statement.

In her cover letter, Melissa wrote about her alignment with the clinic's non-diet and HAES-aligned approach and shared how she admired the way Optimum Intake tailors' services to support not just the child, but the whole family unit. During the interview, she referenced the team's commitment to Ellyn Satter's Division of Responsibility and spoke about how she had seen this model work effectively during one of her university placements. She highlighted her passion for helping families feel less pressure around food and more supported in building long-term confidence.

What really stood out, though, was how Melissa described her interest in learning how to deliver sessions that integrate both nutrition and behaviour change, as she had seen mentioned in Optimum Intake's interview preparation materials. She shared how her own values aligned with the guiding principles of 'client-centred compassionate care' and 'food first, supplement when necessary'. She even mentioned that she'd love to be part of the team contributing to new initiatives and group education, reflecting the clinic's emphasis on teamwork, learning, and innovation.

While another candidate had more clinical experience, Melissa got the job. Why? Because she didn't just show up prepared, she showed up aligned. She demonstrated that she wasn't just looking for *a* job, but *this* job. And that level of insight, research, and values-match made her a clear choice.

Questions That Stood Out

Jason had recently graduated and was interviewing for a generalist role at Optimum Intake. While preparing, he noticed that the clinic had strong services across paediatrics, aged care, and eating disorders, but less content on vegetarian nutrition or sports nutrition, which were two areas he was genuinely passionate about.

Instead of simply hoping he'd be a good fit, Jason came to the interview with curiosity and initiative. He brought a printout of a recent social media post and said, 'I noticed your clinic is doing amazing work in paediatrics and eating disorder care, but I haven't seen much yet in the area of vegetarian nutrition or sports-focused services. Is this something you're looking to expand? And if so, how could I help support that growth?'

The question showed that Jason had done his homework. He wasn't asking for the business to create something for him, he was offering to contribute to an area of potential growth. He spoke about his Honours project on iron intake in adolescent athletes, and how he could bring that lens to support the clinic's younger clients who were active or plant-based eaters. He also showed openness to learning, saying, 'I'd love mentorship in how to blend my interests with the company's client needs.'

What stood out most was Jason's mindset: he wasn't focused on what he could get, he was focused on what he could give. And that's what made him memorable. The leadership team left the interview not just thinking, 'he'd be good in the role', but, 'he's someone who could grow with us'.

Looking Beyond the Pay Cheque

When you're early in your private practice career, it's tempting to weigh every opportunity against the salary figure first. And yes, fair pay matters. But if you make your decision purely on short-term financial gain, you risk missing out on roles that could set you up for far greater rewards in the long run.

Some positions offer something far more valuable than a slightly higher starting rate: mentorship, skill-building, and access to an environment that grows your confidence and capability. These are the roles that compound in value over time. When you choose a workplace that invests in your learning, you're not just trading your hours for dollars, you're building a skillset that can sustain your career for decades.

Ask yourself:

- Will I be learning from experienced dietitians who want to share their knowledge?
- Does this role expose me to varied cases that will challenge and grow my skills?
- Will I have opportunities for feedback, supervision, and professional development?

The best leaders know that initiative and self-awareness are worth more than a flawless CV or perfect academic record. They notice when you prepare well, ask thoughtful questions, and take ownership of your learning. These qualities make you stand out and they're what often lead to promotions, new opportunities, and the trust to take on more responsibility.

In short: choose the role that will stretch you, not just pay you. Because a year in a truly supportive, growth-focused environment can do more for your career than years in a job that only looks good on paper.

Interviewing As the Employer – Finding Your Right Fit

So far in this chapter, we've looked at interviews from the candidate's side, how they can prepare, present, and position themselves for success. But as a private practice owner, you'll often find yourself on the other side of the table. And here's the truth: the quality of your hiring decisions will shape not just your team, but your business's future.

Before you even write a job ad, get crystal clear on exactly what you need. This isn't just 'We need another dietitian', it's defining the role in detail.

Ask yourself:

- What *type* of role is this? (e.g., generalist, niche specialty, community-based, clinic-based)
- What clinical skills, qualifications, and experiences are essential versus 'nice to have'?

- What personal attributes and strengths would make someone thrive here? (e.g., strong communicator, adaptable, values-driven)
- What stage of career would best suit the role? (new graduate eager to learn, or experienced practitioner able to work independently?)

Next, think about your company's values and environment. What do you stand for? How do you work? What's it *really* like to be part of your team? The more honestly you can answer these, the better you'll be at attracting people who are aligned and repelling those who aren't.

Then, define the support and compensation package you're offering. If you're seeking an experienced dietitian, the role will need to offer autonomy, competitive pay, and possibly leadership opportunities. If you're targeting an emerging dietitian, highlight the training, supervision, and structured support you'll provide. What you offer will determine who applies and that's exactly what you want. The goal is not to attract *everyone*, but the *right* ones.

When writing your job advertisement, don't be generic. Use language that reflects your unique company personality and values. Be specific about what the role involves and what kind of person will thrive in it. Include the quirks, the culture, and the things that make your workplace special. The words you use will both attract and filter, so let them do the heavy lifting.

When it comes to shortlisting and interviewing, remember:

- Don't compromise just to fill the seat quickly. The wrong hire can cost you far more than waiting for the right one.

- Be fair and consistent, but also intentional. Only hire someone you genuinely believe will be a good fit for the role and the team.
- Prepare interview questions that will actually give you valuable information. Skip the 'filler' questions you think you're *supposed* to ask. Instead, ask what you *really* want to know about their thinking, their values, their ability to adapt, and how they might handle specific scenarios relevant to your business.
- Be ready to communicate *your* expectations and vision clearly in the interview, so candidates can also assess whether you're the right fit for them.

Hiring is a two-way process. The right match happens when both sides leave the interview feeling confident that the role, the environment, and the expectations are aligned.

Additional key takeaways:

1. *Know what you want* in this season of your life: mentorship, flexibility, niche development, stability, or leadership.
2. Interview with the mindset that you're also assessing the employer.
3. Tailored, authentic applications stand out far more than AI-generated ones.

Hiring Checklist for Private Practice Dietitian Employers

Before You Advertise

- Clearly define the role (generalist, specialty, clinic vs. community work).
- List essential vs. desirable qualifications, skills, and experience.
- Identify personal attributes that will help someone thrive in your workplace.
- Decide what stage of career you're targeting (new grad vs. experienced).
- Outline the support, mentoring, and training you can realistically offer.
- Determine your compensation package (hourly rate/salary, benefits, incentives).
- Reflect on your company values and culture, what makes you unique?
- Draft a job ad that reflects your values, personality, and expectations.

When Shortlisting Candidates

- Review CVs and cover letters for alignment with your role requirements and values.
- Consider both technical skills and interpersonal/ soft skills.
- Look for initiative and genuine interest in your business (research, alignment).

- Eliminate candidates who don't meet essential criteria (don't compromise).

Before the Interview

- Decide who will be in the interview panel (if applicable).
- Prepare 6–8 targeted questions that will give meaningful insight into the candidate's fit.
- Include scenario-based and values-based questions, not just technical ones.
- Review the candidate's application so your questions are personalised.
- Be ready to clearly explain your company's vision, culture, and expectations.

During the Interview

- Create a welcoming environment so the candidate can perform at their best.
- Ask open-ended questions and allow space for discussion.
- Observe not only what they say, but how they say it (confidence, empathy, curiosity).
- Be honest about the role's challenges as well as the benefits.
- Allow time for the candidate to ask you questions (this tells you what they value).

After the Interview

- Review notes and impressions while they're fresh.
- Compare candidates against the defined role, not against each other.
- Consider trial tasks or follow-up conversations if needed.
- Make a decision based on alignment with role requirements, values, and long-term potential — not just "who feels nice".
- Communicate your decision promptly and professionally, offering feedback where possible.

10

Be the Dietitian Practices Want to Keep

In private practice, being a great clinician is only part of the story — to truly thrive, you need to become the kind of team member businesses are proud to invest in and keep.

What if you could confidently grow your career, feel deeply valued in your role, and know exactly how to contribute meaningfully to the success of your team, all while doing work you love?

Many dietitians enter private practice assuming their role is simply to show up, help clients, and document the session. But in private practice, especially in team-based models, that mindset will only take you so far.

Unlike hospital or government roles where your position is funded regardless of your individual output, private practice operates like a finely tuned ecosystem. Every client who attends, every system that runs smoothly, and every dollar earned (or lost) is directly influenced by how each team member contributes.

This chapter matters because your success is deeply linked to how you show up — clinically, yes, but also collaboratively, operationally, and professionally.

You don't have to be a business expert to make a difference. But you do need to understand that being part of a private practice means being part of a business. One that survives and thrives based on how each team member supports the whole, not just their individual work.

When you understand this, you shift from employee to essential. From someone who just does the job, to someone the business can't imagine running without.

Being the kind of team member a practice wants to keep, isn't about perfection or people-pleasing, it's about being invested.

It's about:

- Noticing and fixing a broken process instead of just working around it.
- Being proactive with communication, not just reactive when something goes wrong.
- Offering ideas for how to improve client experience, not just delivering a handout.
- Understanding the numbers that impact business health, attendance, cancellations, average sessions per client and taking accountability for your role in them.

Team members who thrive in private practice are those who take ownership of their impact, stay curious, and commit to learning beyond the clinical. They build trust, deliver value, and contribute to a culture of sustainability, for themselves, their clients, and the business. And in return? They're the ones offered advancement, flexibility, recognition, and long-term career security. Because great practices want to keep great people, especially the ones who help the practice grow.

Sometimes, dietitians unintentionally limit their impact (and opportunities) by thinking too narrowly about their role. Let's look at a few common mindsets that can hold you back and how shifting them can help you contribute, grow and thrive.

'That's not my job, the owner should be responsible for that'

It's true, business owners carry a lot of responsibility. But the best workplaces don't run on hierarchy alone — they thrive on collaboration. When you see yourself as part of the solution, not just someone clocking in and out, you become an invaluable team member. Showing initiative, supporting the systems, and thinking about how your actions impact the team and the business doesn't mean taking on everything. It means showing up with a mindset that says, *'How can I help this business succeed, so I can succeed within it?'* That mindset doesn't go unnoticed, it builds trust, loyalty, and long-term opportunities.

'I'm not good at marketing or business'

You don't need a business degree to be effective in private practice, but you do need curiosity and a willingness to learn. Business and marketing in a healthcare setting often just means being able to speak about what you do in a clear, relatable way. It means understanding how your work contributes to client retention, reputation, and outcomes. You're already marketing when you follow up with a client kindly, when you share helpful information, when you help someone feel seen and supported. That's where marketing in private practice starts. The rest is learnable and we're better clinicians when we understand how the business supports the care.

'I'm just here to see clients'

And that's an incredibly important part of your role, but it's not the *only* part in private practice. The reality is your ability to keep seeing clients and to be paid fairly for it depends on the business staying sustainable. That includes reducing cancellations, supporting admin, helping the team meet service delivery targets, and maintaining strong therapeutic relationships with clients. The more you understand how your role fits into the bigger picture, the more empowered you become to influence your own success, job security, and even your earning potential. When the business thrives, you do too.

When you step into your role with the mindset that you're not just part of the business, but a driver of its success, everything changes. You stand out. You create opportunities. You become the kind of team member a business wants to invest in, promote, and keep for the long haul. And the best part? Those same actions that help the practice thrive will also accelerate your own growth, security, and career satisfaction.

Here's how:

Greater job security and retention
When you contribute meaningfully to a private practice, beyond your clinical skills, you become a team member the business wants to keep. Showing that you understand how your work impacts the business helps build trust, loyalty, and long-term opportunities. Dietitians who are proactive, reliable, and aligned with the practice's values are more likely to be retained during times of change, offered permanent contracts, and included in future planning decisions.

More opportunities for growth and promotion
The more value you add, the more visible your strengths become and so do your opportunities. Whether it's stepping into a mentoring role, leading a niche service stream, contributing to internal projects, or representing the clinic at external events, private practices notice and reward initiative. Growth doesn't just mean climbing a ladder, it could mean shaping your own career direction within the business.

Clearer career progression
When you track your contribution and understand your impact on clients, team systems, or business outcomes you're in a better position to map out your development. You can identify the skills to build next, co-create a professional development plan with your team leader, and pursue structured pathways within the practice. Rather than waiting passively for someone to promote

you, you'll feel equipped to advocate for your progression with evidence and confidence.

Stronger client relationships and outcomes
When you feel connected to your workplace, supported by systems, and motivated to contribute, this flows through to your client care. You're more present, more confident, and more consistent and clients can feel that. They're more likely to stay engaged, attend sessions, and achieve their goals when they feel part of a seamless and professional experience. Your clinical outcomes improve, and your reputation grows.

Ability to negotiate better pay or conditions based on performance
In private practice, demonstrating your value gives you leverage. When you can show how your work contributes to business success whether through client outcomes, retention, referrals, or innovation you're in a stronger position to negotiate compensation, request flexible working conditions, or step into higher-paying roles. You'll be able to approach these conversations with clarity, data, and confidence.

> *'Average team members show up. Exceptional ones step up.'*

We've talked about how contributing beyond your clinical role can build trust, create opportunities, and accelerate your growth but sometimes the best way to understand the impact is to see it in action.

The following three stories show how different approaches to the same workplace can lead to very different outcomes, both for the individual and the business.

The New Grad Who Stood Out

When Mia joined a private practice straight out of university, she was open about her lack of experience but had a genuine enthusiasm for learning. From her first week, she didn't just passively follow instructions, she asked thoughtful questions about how the clinic worked, what systems were in place, and how she could be involved in different projects and help other team members when she had a spare moment.

Rather than waiting to be told what to do, Mia offered questions about WHY things are done a specific way which prompted reflection and created opportunities for the team to generate new ideas to tweak and improve communication templates, volunteered to help write blog post series to promote the clinic's niche services, and regularly checked in with her team leader to ask how she was tracking. She didn't try to act like she knew everything instead, she showed humility, initiative, and a willingness to grow.

Within six months, her calendar was booked solid. Clients responded to her clarity and care and would often sing her praises through formal and informal opportunities. Her team respected her reliability and positivity. By the end of her third year, she was promoted to a team leader role, not because she had more years of experience, but because she had earned trust, proven her alignment with the business, and contributed to its growth from the inside.

The System Saboteur

Ben had been part of a private practice team for several years and was known for being a strong clinician. But over time, his resistance to change began to weigh on the team. Whenever a new process was introduced a different note-taking tool, a revised handover format, or updates to the intake procedure, Ben would roll his eyes, refuse to use the tools, or complain to newer team members about how "things used to be done in previous workplaces".

At first, the leadership team tried to accommodate him, hoping he'd come around. But his negativity started to impact morale. New grads felt unsure whether to follow the systems or side with Ben's opinions. Admin found it difficult to manage communication inconsistencies. The clinical director noticed that while the clinical work and support for clients remained intact the relational impact on the team and business became too great. After a number of discussions, it was decided that for Ben to achieve this next goal in his career that couldn't be something that was possible to offer in his current workplace. So, with a plan in place Ben was supported to pursue other positions that were better aligned with his future plans and passion area.

With a positive reference highlighting his clinical skills and preferred way of working, Ben was able to move on from his current role in the business and pursue his next career step elsewhere and a new team member was able to step into the role, join the team and continue innovating and moving forward with the business. Transparency in aligned values and when things change, discussing it openly allows for both parties to find what they are looking for without forcing a match that is unaligned.

The Intrapreneurial Thinker

Sophie, a dietitian with a growing caseload in paediatrics, began noticing a pattern: a high number of last-minute cancellations from parents. Instead of venting to colleagues or blaming clients, she became curious. She brought her concerns to supervision and together decided they needed more quantitative data to understand the situation in more detail. Sophie reached out to the admin team to look at the booking data and discovered that many of the cancellations were coming from new clients who hadn't received adequate communication between their intake and first appointment.

Rather than hand the problem off, Sophie offered to help co-design a new intake workflow. She worked closely with admin to draft a welcome email sequence, a pre-appointment questionnaire, and an FAQ sheet for parents nervous about their first session. She also added a "What to Expect" section to her bio and created a short video introducing herself.

Within two months, the no-show and cancellation rate dropped by 40%. The admin team felt empowered, the client experience improved dramatically, and Sophie's initiative was praised in team meetings. She didn't just raise a problem; she helped solve it.

That's what intrapreneurship looks like: noticing issues, bringing a collaborative mindset, and improving the business for everyone involved.

Value Contribution Pyramid

From Clinician to Intrapreneur

The Value Contribution Pyramid is a simple way to visualise how your role in private practice can grow, starting with delivering great clinical care, then adding layers of collaboration, initiative, and innovation that make you not just a good team member, but an irreplaceable one.

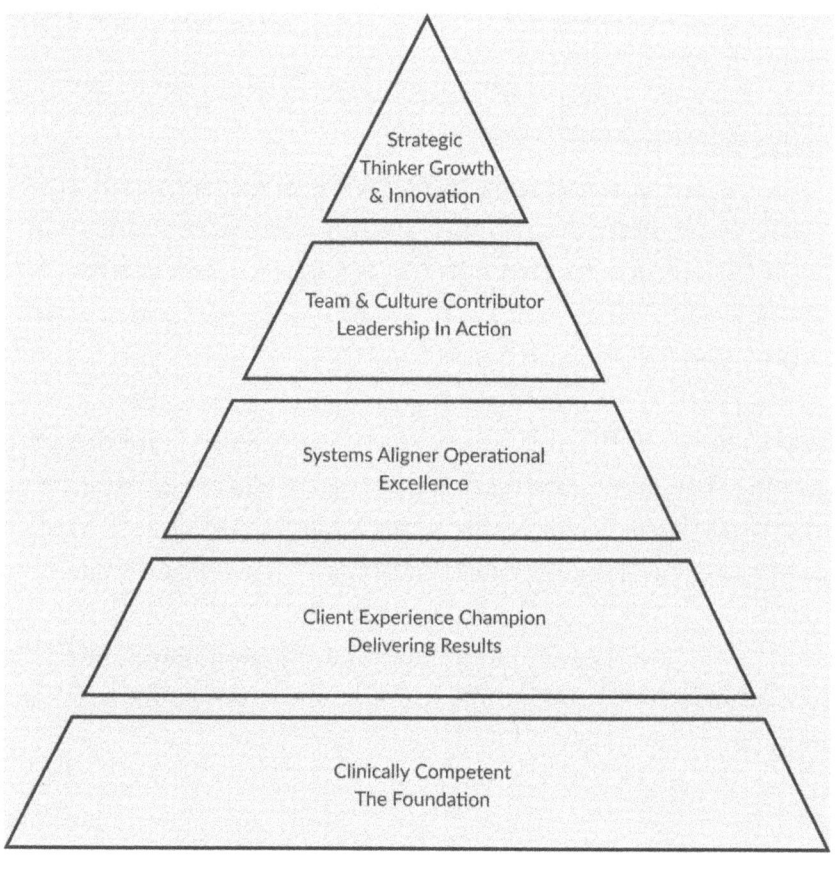

Image 2: The Value Contribution Pyramid

Tier 5: Strategic Thinker (Top of Pyramid) – Practice Growth & Innovation.
- Identifies service gaps and proposes new offerings
- Supports marketing initiatives and builds referral relationships
- Contributes to strategic planning or leads projects
- Champions team development and mentors others
- Thinks like an owner, considers sustainability and long-term impact

Tier 4: Team & Culture Contributor – Leadership in Action.
- Supports a culture of accountability and professionalism
- Provides feedback constructively and receives it openly
- Proactively solves problems instead of waiting to be asked
- Helps onboard and support new team members
- Participates in team meetings with ideas, not just attendance

Tier 3: Systems Aligner – Operational Excellence.
- Follows practice systems, policies, and procedures consistently
- Completes reports, admin tasks, and documentation on time
- Communicates effectively with admin, managers, and other disciplines
- Understands the "why" behind processes and contributes to improvements

Tier 2: Client Experience Champion – Delivering Results.
- Provides exceptional, client-centred care
- Offers clear treatment plans with appropriate follow-up
- Manages time well during sessions

- Improves client retention and outcomes through structured care

Tier 1: Clinically Competent – The Foundation.
- Applies evidence-based nutrition knowledge
- Works within scope of practice
- Seeks supervision and ongoing learning
- Demonstrates professionalism and ethical practice

How to Use This Pyramid:

- Reflect on which tier you spend most of your time in.
- Set a goal to move up one level over the next quarter.
- Use this model in supervision or performance reviews to guide professional development.

Here are three practical ways you can put this chapter into action and strengthen both your role and your confidence in private practice.

1. Reflect on and list the ways you add value to your workplace beyond clinical skills.
2. Ask your manager what outcomes you're responsible for and track them.
3. Commit to improving one "non-clinical" skill: communication, marketing, systems, or teamwork.

11

Burnout Isn't Inevitable – Build a Career That Lasts

What if the reason so many dietitians burn out isn't because private practice is unsustainable but because no one taught us how to make it sustainable?

What if you could build a thriving private practice career without sacrificing your mental health?

What if you stopped normalising overwhelm and emotional exhaustion, and saw burnout not as your inevitable fate, but as a clear signal to redesign your work life?

Imagine protecting your energy in a way that allows you to love your work for the long term, creating a career that feels sustainable, purposeful, and deeply rewarding. Burnout is not a personal failure. It's not because you're not resilient enough, tough enough, or organised enough. Burnout is a predictable outcome of being in a system that doesn't teach dietitians how to manage the emotional labour, invisible workload, or the mental stories we tell ourselves about what we 'should' be doing.

1. Burnout: A state of emotional, physical, and mental exhaustion caused by excessive and prolonged stress, especially in work contexts.
2. Emotional Labour: The internal effort required to manage your emotions and present a calm, compassionate front, even when depleted.
3. Healthy Professional Identity: A grounded, flexible mindset where you recognise your role in outcomes, but don't take full responsibility for every client's progress.

Many dietitians enter private practice driven by passion and purpose, but quickly find themselves overwhelmed not just by the number of clients, but by all the things no one prepared them for:

- The heaviness of caring deeply about people's struggles
- The guilt of charging for your time when someone is in need
- The internal conflict of wanting to do more, but having no capacity left
- The blurred lines between work and life, especially when you're self-employed or working from home
- The pressure to 'do it all' market your services, manage admin, stay clinically up to date, write reports, respond to emails, build your business… all while being a caring, compassionate, evidence-based clinician

BURNOUT ISN'T INEVITABLE – BUILD A CAREER THAT LASTS

Burnout often creeps in silently disguised as over-responsibility, people-pleasing, or perfectionism. You may still be showing up and doing the work, but inside you're running on fumes. And because our profession is so focused on service and care, many dietitians internalise this struggle. They think *'Maybe I'm not cut out for this'*, when really, the problem isn't *you*, it's the lack of preparation and support.

This chapter helps you reset those expectations. It helps you take a step back from the noise and ask:

- What's mine to carry, and what's not?
- What boundaries need strengthening?
- What internal beliefs need challenging?
- What systems do I need in place to protect my energy, not just my calendar?

You'll learn the most common contributors to burnout in private practice and practical, real-life strategies to rewire your work patterns for sustainability. This isn't about hustle culture or spa days. It's about designing a professional life you don't need to escape from.

Burnout is not inevitable but without intention, it is likely. With the right tools, mindset, and support, you can create a version of private practice that energises you instead of draining you.

Before we can talk about preventing or recovering from burnout, we have to address the beliefs that keep it alive in the first place. These quiet assumptions and internal scripts often convince us to push harder, avoid boundaries, or delay making changes until 'later.' But left unchecked, they don't just keep us stuck, they quietly speed up the burnout process.

Let's unpack a few of the most common ones and explore how to reframe them into something far more sustainable.

I just need to push through — it'll get better eventually.

This is one of the most common and dangerous beliefs dietitians hold. While persistence is a strength, pushing through without changing the underlying causes only leads to deeper fatigue. Burnout doesn't usually resolve on its own. Without addressing the root issues like emotional labour, perfectionism, blurred boundaries, or lack of recovery time things rarely improve. In fact, they often worsen. True sustainability comes from working differently, not just working harder.

'If I set boundaries, I'll come across as rude or let people down'

Many dietitians, especially those early in their careers, struggle with the idea that setting limits means being difficult, unhelpful, or selfish. But boundaries are not about pushing people away; they're about protecting your capacity to keep showing up sustainably. If you're constantly saying yes to last-minute requests, replying to emails late at night, or squeezing in 'quick' favours, you're training others to expect that, at the cost of your well-being.

Avoiding boundaries may keep the peace temporarily, but it leads to resentment, exhaustion, and often burnout. What needs to shift is not just your behaviour, but your beliefs about what it means to be 'helpful'. Boundaries communicate professionalism, self-respect, and clarity. They are a sign of someone who takes their role and their energy seriously. Saying 'no' or 'not right now' isn't letting someone down. It's showing up in a way that's honest, considered, and ultimately more effective in the long term.

'I'm too early in my career to worry about burnout'

The truth is, early-career clinicians are often at *higher* risk of burnout, not lower. You're navigating steep learning curves, impostor syndrome, and often saying yes to everything out of fear you won't get another opportunity. But prevention is far easier than recovery. Learning to set limits, protect your energy, and manage your expectations early on builds resilience. You deserve to create a career that lasts, not one you have to recover from later.

According to research by the Black Dog Institute, burnout in clinicians can manifest as emotional fragility, physical symptoms, memory loss, and withdrawal and younger professionals especially those in private practice are particularly at risk.

If burnout chips away at our energy, clarity, and connection, then protecting ourselves from it does far more than just 'help us cope'. It actively strengthens our ability to thrive, both as clinicians and as people. When we prioritise boundaries, recovery, and sustainable ways of working, we don't just avoid the worst-case scenario, we unlock the best-case benefits that ripple into every part of our professional and personal lives.

Here's what that can look like:

Greater self-awareness around personal and professional limits
Burnout often sneaks in when we don't know or ignore our boundaries. Developing self-awareness helps you recognise early signs of overload, understand what drains or replenishes your energy, and set realistic expectations of yourself. It also empowers you to identify what is truly yours to carry in your work and what needs to be let go. This kind of awareness is foundational for healthy, long-term practice and it's a skill you'll carry with you throughout your entire career.

Stronger emotional resilience
When you're supported with the right mindset, boundaries, and systems, you're better equipped to handle the inevitable emotional ups and downs of client care. Resilience doesn't mean avoiding hard things, it means moving through them without crumbling. Building emotional resilience allows you to care deeply without becoming consumed, and to recover more quickly when challenges arise.

Reduced fatigue and cynicism
Chronic overwork and compassion fatigue can leave even the most passionate dietitians feeling numb, detached, or resentful. When you put in place strategies to protect your time and emotional energy like saying no without guilt, delegating tasks, or stepping away when needed you prevent the slow buildup of resentment that leads to cynicism. Instead, you stay connected to the meaning and joy in your work.

Increased longevity and joy in your private practice career
Private practice is a marathon, not a sprint. When you intentionally design a work life that honours your limits, your values, and your

capacity, you build a business that's not only sustainable but genuinely enjoyable. You'll be able to grow your impact without sacrificing your health or relationships, and your business will evolve with you as your life changes.

Improved client outcomes through more present and connected care
Your ability to be attuned, compassionate, and creative with clients depends on your own regulation and well-being. Burnout dulls your intuition, reduces your patience, and impairs your problem-solving. But when you're well-rested, supported, and working within your limits, you're more present, curious, and collaborative, which leads to better client outcomes and stronger therapeutic relationships.

> *'You are not required to set yourself on fire to keep others warm.' – Unknown*

Now that we've explored why burnout happens and what's at stake if it's left unchecked, it's time to turn our focus to what actually works in preventing and recovering from it.

These stories show exactly how dietitians have made those changes, often starting from a place of exhaustion, and rebuilt their work in a way that protects their energy, reignites their purpose, and makes private practice something they can see themselves thriving in for years to come.

The Early Career Dietitian from Drowning to Grounded

Renae graduated with high hopes and an almost full calendar. Excited and eager to prove herself, she accepted a full-time caseload at a busy multidisciplinary private practice where she was the only dietitian. But there was a problem: she had no supervision, no mentor, and no idea how to manage the emotional load that came with her new role. Every client's story hit her deeply. She ruminated over sessions, questioning whether she said the right thing, if she helped enough, or if the client even liked her. She skipped lunch most days, stayed up late writing notes and reports, and constantly felt like she was falling behind.

Despite enjoying seeing her clients, she began to dread work. She started googling other career options and quietly wondered if she'd made a mistake going into dietetics.

The turning point came when a colleague gently suggested supervision. Renae attended her first session reluctantly, expecting judgment. Instead, she found relief. Over time, she learned how to separate her self-worth from client outcomes, how to emotionally 'debrief' after intense sessions, and how to protect her time with better boundaries. She dropped back to four days a week, started eating lunch again, and began to reconnect with the part of her that *wanted* to help people not because she had to prove something, but because it genuinely brought her joy.

'I didn't need to change careers, I just needed to feel supported in the one I had,' Renae now says.

The High Achiever's Unrelenting Standards

Grace had been in private practice for five years. She had a full calendar, glowing testimonials, and colleagues who admired her work ethic. But inside, Grace was struggling. She believed that to be valuable, she had to be perfect, never say no, never make a mistake, never rest. She accepted every referral, squeezed in extra clients, and apologised if she ever took a day off. Even during holidays, she checked emails, worried about her clients, and replayed sessions in her head.

Eventually, Grace began to emotionally detach. She no longer felt joy in her work. She smiled in sessions, but internally, she was flat. She questioned whether she was helping anyone at all. She told herself, *'Maybe I'm just burned out. Maybe I don't care anymore.'*

But deep down, Grace *did* care. She just had nothing left to give.

A turning point came during a reflective supervision session when Grace uncovered the belief driving her overwork: *'I am responsible for every client outcome.'* This belief was crushing her.

Through accessing personal therapy and coaching, Grace learned to challenge her unrelenting standards. She realised that holding high standards didn't mean sacrificing herself. She began saying no to clients who weren't a fit, took her first real holiday without guilt, and returned to her values: connection, curiosity, and collaboration. Her sessions became lighter, her outcomes improved, and most importantly she started liking herself again.

> *'Letting go of perfection didn't make me less of a dietitian. It made me a better one.'*

The Private Practice Redesign

Ben had been running his own practice for four years. From the outside, everything looked great: a booked-out calendar, strong referral streams, and glowing client reviews. But Ben was exhausted. He worked evenings to accommodate 'just one more client,' caught up on admin on weekends, and didn't remember the last time he took a full day off without checking his inbox.

He kept telling himself, *'I'll rest when things settle down.'* But they never did.

One night, after staying up past midnight finalising reports, Ben hit a wall, 'I can't keep doing this.' He knew he didn't want to quit, he *loved* working with his clients but the version of private practice he had created was unsustainable.

So, he got honest with himself. He reviewed his calendar and redesigned his entire week:

- No more evening sessions
- Admin time was built into his workday
- Protected supervision sessions were booked monthly
- Consults were shortened and priced accordingly
- He started outsourcing some tasks to a virtual assistant

At first, the shift felt uncomfortable like he was being 'lazy' or 'less available'. But within a few months, everything changed. Ben had energy again. He brought more presence to his sessions, had space for creative ideas, and even started mentoring newer clinicians.

'I didn't quit private practice, I redesigned it. And now I can actually see myself doing this for the next 10 years.'

Now that we've explored the why and the how, here are a few simple, practical steps you can start applying straight away:

- Complete a Therapist Belief Scale to identify maladaptive thought patterns contributing to burnout. These scales are valuable tools for helping to understand how therapists' beliefs influence their practice, treatment decisions, and client outcomes. You can Google different ones and then take them to your supervisor to unpack.
- Design your non-negotiables: Define what boundaries, breaks, and lifestyle factors help you feel safe, grounded, and energised at work.
- Establish a burnout prevention plan: Include support (supervision), structure (admin breaks), and strategies for managing emotional labour.

Burnout Prevention Plan – Sample Template

Name: _____

Date: _____

1. Support – Who and what will help me maintain perspective and prevent isolation?

   - Supervision/Coaching:
     - Frequency: _____
     - Supervisor/Coach: _____
     - Focus areas: _____
       _____
       _____
       _____

   - Peer Support / Networking:
     - Who I can reach out to when I need professional encouragement:
       _____
     - How I will keep these connections active (e.g., monthly coffee catch-ups, online forums):
       _____

   - Personal Support Network:
     - Friends/family I can lean on for emotional support outside of work:
       _____

2. Structure – How I will organise my work week to protect my energy and prevent overload

- Admin Breaks Built into My Week:
    - Time slots: _____
    - Tasks to complete during admin time: _____
    _____

- Boundaries Around Session Load:
    - Maximum number of client sessions per day:
    _____
    - Minimum buffer time between sessions:
    _____

- Scheduled Downtime:
    - Days off each week: _____
    - Annual leave planned: _____

3. Strategies for Managing Emotional Labour – How I will process and release the emotional weight of my work

- Post-Session Reset Routine:
    - Quick activities to 'clear the slate' before the next client (e.g., deep breathing, short walk, journaling):
    _____

- End-of-Day Debrief:
    - How I'll reflect and let go of the workday: _____
    _____
    _____

- Ongoing Self-Care Practices:
    - Daily: _____
    - Weekly: _____
    - Monthly: _____

Commitment Statement:

"I commit to protecting my energy, seeking support when needed, and maintaining the structures that help me thrive in my private practice career."

Signature: _____
Date: _____

Don't Let Your Niche Define You – Grow Your Skills, Not Just Your Title

You are more than your niche. While it may shape your early steps, it doesn't have to limit your long-term path.

There's a common belief among early-career dietitians that niching down is the golden rule of success. You're told to pick a niche early, become known for it, and build your whole brand around it. But here's the truth most experienced private practitioners eventually learn: you are going to change.

Your interests will change. Your confidence will grow. You'll have new life experiences, client conversations, and professional insights that shift how you want to work and who you want to work with. And if your identity is too tightly wrapped around one niche, you may end up feeling trapped rather than empowered.

Private practice doesn't have to be a straight line. In fact, for most dietitians, it isn't.

What matters most isn't your niche, it's your skills, your values, your capacity to learn, and your ability to connect with clients in a meaningful way.

Unfortunately, many dietitians hesitate to evolve because they've anchored their identity to their niche. They fear that a pivot means starting over, confusing their audience, or losing credibility. But staying stuck in a niche that no longer aligns is what drains your energy, dulls your impact, and creates resentment.

Sometimes, your decision to pivot comes from curiosity and growth. But other times, it's driven by external realities like shifts in funding models, government initiatives, or a saturated market that forces you to adapt. You may not have planned to change your focus, but change becomes necessary to stay relevant, serve clients who can afford your services, and keep your business sustainable. Whether by choice or by necessity, change is part of the private practice journey.

In my own journey, I didn't start out with a specialty. I began with a mix of casual roles: research assistant, paediatrics, oncology, diabetes, respiratory, public health and started a private practice alongside still working in my retail job in a shoe shop. Over time, I stepped into an eating disorder role with zero experience in this area, just a desire to learn. That position reshaped my career. I've since built two private practice businesses, one grounded in generalist care and the other in eating disorder treatment. My evolution wasn't linear, it was responsive, expansive, and aligned with my values and the changing landscape.

And this is what I want you to remember: you don't have to choose between breadth and depth. You can have both. You can shift and grow. You can follow curiosity and stay strategic.

This chapter encourages you to:

- See your niche as a launchpad, not a life sentence
- View change as a sign of professional maturity, not failure
- Build a clinical identity rooted in *who you are*, not just *what you do*

Because when you grow in alignment with your values, your business will grow with you.

Niche: A specialised area of practice, often based on population, condition, or modality.

Professional Identity: How you see yourself and your purpose in your role as a clinician.

Transferable Skills: Skills that can be applied across populations or settings (e.g., counselling, critical thinking, communication).

Shifting your focus or redefining your niche can feel exciting, but it often comes with a wave of doubts and "what ifs" that can keep you stuck.

Let's address some of the most common worries so they don't hold you back from making the changes you know are right for you.

'But I've built my whole identity around this niche'

It's normal to feel attached to what you've built. You've invested time, energy, and heart into becoming known in a specific area. But your professional identity isn't just your niche, it's your *values*, your *voice*, and your *way of working*. Those things can carry across client groups and evolve over time. Think of it as re-aligning your brand, not abandoning it. Your brand becomes richer when it reflects your current passion and purpose.

'Won't I lose clients or referrals if I change focus?'

Maybe. But that's not always a bad thing. Some people may no longer be the right fit and that creates space for the clients who *are*. With clear messaging, intentional updates, and professional communication, you won't confuse your audience you'll guide them. You don't lose your current skills and knowledge, which means you CAN still service your current customers, while actively promoting another area that are now be more interested in. Change doesn't mean rejection. It means refinement. And often, your most aligned clients find you *after* the pivot.

'I don't feel qualified to change areas of practice.'

It's okay to feel unsure. Every new stage brings a learning curve that doesn't mean you're unqualified, it means you're evolving. You don't need to know everything before you begin. What you *do* need is a growth mindset, strong supervision, and a commitment to safe, evidence-informed practice. Most importantly, you're allowed to *start* learning your niche didn't appear overnight, and neither will your next one.

> *'Most private practice dietitians change or expand their niche within the first 3–5 years. Your path is allowed to evolve.'*

When you approach a niche change with clarity and intention, the rewards can be significant—both for your career and your wellbeing. Let's explore the key benefits you can expect when you give yourself permission to evolve.

Freedom to shape your career on your terms, not just market demand

When your niche isn't your only professional identity, you give yourself the flexibility to grow without needing to start over. You can adapt your practice based on your passions, your lifestyle, or your changing client base. You remain in the driver's seat not boxed in by outdated expectations or external definitions of success.

Increased job satisfaction as your interests evolve over time

Boredom and misalignment are common reasons dietitians burn out. When you give yourself permission to follow your curiosity and refine your practice areas, work becomes more energising and meaningful. You'll feel more connected to your clients and more fulfilled in your day-to-day role because it reflects who you are *now*, not just who you were at the start.

Broader skillset and more diversified income opportunities

A flexible niche means developing a wider range of clinical skills, business tools, and referral networks. This opens new doors; workshops, courses, program development, consulting, or mentorship. You're not just building depth in one area, you're building breadth across your career. That diversity creates stability and creativity in your work.

Greater resilience when funding models, demand, or passions shift

Whether it's Medicare rules, NDIS changes, or industry trends, external factors will always evolve. A dietitian whose entire business is tied to one funding stream or one client population, is more vulnerable when those shifts occur. When you've built adaptability into your business model, you can pivot without panic because you've prepared for evolution, not resisted it.

A career identity rooted in values and growth, not just labels

You are more than your job title. When you connect your work to your personal values, curiosity, compassion, and impact your professional identity becomes stronger and more sustainable. You'll feel more confident in navigating change because you're anchored in something deeper than a niche: your purpose.

'Your niche should serve your growth, not limit it.'

I've taken more than a few detours on my way to finding my place in dietetics, and I wouldn't change them for anything. These stories, pulled from my own career path, highlight the different ways you can explore, grow, and carve out a role that truly fits you. The first one begins with my early days in dietetics, when variety, not specialisation, turned out to be my greatest asset.

The Generalist Foundation

In my first year after university, I didn't have a clear direction and looking back now, that worked in my favour. Not that I was aware of it at the time, because there was this perceived pressure to find a full-time job, figure out 'what you want to do', and get a 'safe and secure' position. There was very little help or guidance post-university to actually *find* a job. I was interviewing alongside several others from my cohort, applying for the same jobs. It felt overwhelmingly competitive, like there was this rush to get something, *anything*, within the first couple of months after receiving our graduation marks.

I was eventually successful in finding work a few days a week in a paediatric outpatient clinic, plus doing some research assistant work on the side, still picking up shifts at my retail job in a shoe shop, and simultaneously launching my very first private practice. I wasn't focused on one area of nutrition. Instead, I was saying yes to a variety of opportunities partly out of interest, partly out of necessity.

It wasn't glamorous or particularly strategic, but it gave me something incredibly valuable: perspective. Again, not that I completely identified it at the time or even realised how helpful it would later be, it was just the type of work I could find as a dietitian. I was exposed to different client needs, different systems, and different team environments. I saw what I liked (and what I didn't), what lit me up, and what left me feeling flat. I got to sample the buffet before committing to a main course.

Looking back, those seemingly random roles helped me understand the pace and structure that suited me. They allowed me to develop foundational skills like adaptability, communication, and time management. That early generalist experience became the grounding force that allowed me to later specialise because I knew who I was, how I worked best, and what kind of clients I could support most effectively. And more importantly, it showed me the sector I found most rewarding as a dietitian private practice.

A Career-Defining Pivot

After spending a few years floating between clinical roles from oncology to diabetes to public health I was still unsure of where I wanted to land. I saw a job ad for a two-day-a-week early intervention role in eating disorders. I had no eating disorder experience, aside from a one-hour lecture at university, but something about it sparked my curiosity.

I applied. I got the job. And I had no idea what I was walking into.

I was thrown into a steep learning curve — complex clients, including conducting family therapy sessions for eating disorders; a new language, which back then was the beginning of *The Non-Diet Approach* by Rick Kausman; and confronting emotions from both my clients and myself when supporting them. I could have easily given up. But I didn't. I leaned into upskilling through courses and workshops, learnt from our team of mental health social workers and psychologists, and engaged in regular supervision. I connected with other professionals who inspired me. I gradually built my confidence and learned to trust my instincts.

That one decision to try something completely outside of my comfort zone working in eating disorders ended up being the turning point in my career. Eating disorder work gave me purpose, challenged me to evolve, and introduced me to the Non-Diet Approach, Health At Every Size™, Maudsley Based Family Therapy (MFBT), Cognitive Behavioural Therapy – Enhanced (CBT-E), Acceptance and Commitment Therapy (ACT), counselling skills, and so much more, which went on to become a core part of how I practice. It also showed me what was possible when you stop waiting to feel 'ready' and instead start saying yes to learning.

Balancing Breadth and Depth Through Business Growth

While I found my niche in eating disorders, I remained committed to serving a wide range of people across all ages and health conditions in our local community. I didn't want to be limited in the impact food has to just one area of healthcare, and I knew that I couldn't serve everyone myself. I knew that building a team could help balance my passion with sustainability. So, while I continued with my passion area of eating disorders (and later went on to building a private practice specialising in this field), I continued to grow Optimum Intake Dietitians. I created a space for both generalist care and specialised services.

This decision changed everything.

I hired team members with a diverse range of interests — paediatrics, aged care, disability nutrition, sports nutrition, chronic disease, and so on — and I let them grow in the directions that felt aligned for them. Some team members entered with a niche, while others discovered theirs along the way. Some switched teams or transitioned to leadership roles. We built pathways, not boxes.

This flexibility allowed us to weather external challenges like the COVID-19 pandemic, changing government funding, policy shifts, and market saturation. Because we weren't dependent on a single niche or referral stream, we could pivot when needed, diversify our services, and attract a wider range of clients. It also meant I didn't have to know everything about everything I had a team of experts who each brought something unique to the table.

Over time, this approach not only made the business more resilient, it gave our team room to grow, evolve, and stay engaged in their careers.

> If you're feeling the pull to evolve your career or simply curious about what else might be possible, here are three practical actions you can take to start moving forward without having to overhaul everything at once.
>
> 1. Reflect on whether your current niche still energises and excites you.
> 2. Identify 1–2 adjacent areas of interest that align with your values.
> 3. Take one step: enrol in a workshop, start learning about a new area, or speak to your supervisor about expansion opportunities.

Book Wrap-Up

From Confusion to Confidence!

If you've made it to this point, congratulations. You've just invested in building not just your skills, but your future.

This book was never about teaching you one way to 'do' private practice. It was about helping you realise that there is no one right way except the way that aligns with who you are and what you want. You've explored everything from getting your first job and pricing with purpose, to managing burnout and building a long-term career. You've unpacked what it means to be a valuable team member, a leader, and a confident practitioner even when you're still learning.

Now it's your turn to take what you've learned and apply it.

Reflect on what resonated most. Which chapters challenged you? Which ones lit a fire? Go back and re-read them when you need clarity. Use the worksheets and tools. Share this book with a peer. Talk about what you're learning. Seek supervision for your clinical skills and a business coach for your business skills. Ask better questions. Make braver moves.

The truth is, you don't need permission from anyone else to elevate your career. You get to define success. You get to write your own rules. And with every decision you make — how you price, how you market, how you speak to clients, how you structure your week — you're designing your private practice.

So let it be one that excites you.
Let it be one that grows with you.
Let it be one that reminds you, every single day, why you became a dietitian in the first place.

And if you're ready to keep growing, don't do it alone. Consider investing in a business coach who can help fast-track your progress, keep you accountable, and support you as you step into your next season. I'd love to help you do exactly that.

Reach out to me at Elevated Dietetics or connect with me directly to learn more about how we can work together.

Your journey is just beginning. And you're more ready than you think.

Let's keep elevating.
—Jodie

About the Author

Jodie Sheraton grew up on the Central Coast of New South Wales, just an hour north of Sydney, where weekends were spent at the beach, on the tennis court, or helping her grandparents on their farms. Surrounded by fresh produce and a family that valued hard work, she developed a love for food and an entrepreneurial spirit early on—running a fruit and vegetable stall in her driveway and mowing lawns for elderly neighbours with her brother.

In school, Jodie's interests blended science and creativity. She loved hospitality and cooking but knew a chef's kitchen wasn't the right fit. Instead, she pursued a Bachelor of Health Sciences (Nutrition and Dietetics) at the University of Newcastle, later becoming a Credentialled Eating Disorder Dietitian. Competitive tennis in her teenage years had already shown her the power of fuelling for performance, but it wasn't until her third year of university that she fully realised the scope of a dietitian's impact—and she knew she had found her path.

Her career began with a series of casual positions, until a maternity leave role in early intervention for eating disorders changed everything. Learning the Non-Diet Approach from Dr Rick Kausman reshaped her philosophy as a dietitian and became the foundation of her business values.

Jodie launched her private practice in her first year after graduation—a bold step that came with a steep learning curve. With little business experience, she had to learn quickly. Over time, she grew from a solo clinician to an employer, trainer, and leader of leaders, eventually building a team of more than 40. Along the way, she invested heavily in her own growth, seeking out business and leadership coaching to ensure her company operated with clarity, integrity, and excellence.

Today, Jodie is a recognised leader in Australian dietetics. She has served as Advocacy Leader for the Dietitians Australia Eating Disorders Interest Group (EDIG) and as Convenor of the Dietitians in Private Sector Interest Group (DIPSIG). She is a sought-after speaker at national events, including the Dietitians Australia National Conference and Dietitian Connection's Dietitians Unite, where she inspires clinicians to elevate their practice, embrace business acumen, and create meaningful impact.

Outside of work, Jodie is happiest on the tennis court, in her garden, walking her Labrador, Millie, or cheering on her boys at basketball and tennis. She treasures beach days, family dinners, and quiet moments with a good podcast or Netflix series.

ABOUT THE AUTHOR

Through her company, Elevated Dietetics, Jodie's mission is to help dietitians thrive in private by growing their services, teams, and confidence. She empowers practitioners to elevate their influence, impact, and income—while intentionally designing a business and lifestyle that feels purposeful and sustainable.

In the next decade, Jodie hopes to be remembered as the dietitian who wasn't afraid to go first, who offered others a seat at the table, and who worked tirelessly to raise the standards and possibilities for the profession.

Connect with Jodie:
Email: jodie@elevateddietetics.com.au
Websites: www.elevateddietetics.com.au
Instagram: @elevated_dietetics

Offers

As a reader of *The Confident Dietitian*, I want to make sure you're not just inspired but that you're equipped with the tools, resources, and support you need to take the next step in your private practice journey. Here's how you can continue your journey with Elevated Dietetics:

1. Free Business Plan Template
A practical, easy-to-follow framework to help you map out your private practice vision, strategy, and action steps. Download a beautifully designed and intentional business plan template, completely free from the Elevated Dietetics website. It's the exact framework I use to guide private practice dietitians in mapping out their services, pricing, goals, and growth strategy. Think of it as your compass to build a business with clarity and confidence, without overwhelm.

2. Get It Done Strategy Session
Feeling stuck, overwhelmed, or unsure how to move forward? A focused 90-minute one-on-one session designed to help you *cut through the noise* and move forward with confidence. The **Get It Done** session is a laser-focused, one-on-one strategy call where

you bring your current business challenge, and you'll walk away with:

- Renewed **clarity** from a fresh, experienced perspective
- Rebuilt **confidence** in your decision-making
- A clear **action plan** with prioritised, actionable next steps
- Regain **momentum** and **focus** on your business.

These sessions offer the reflective space, accountability, and expert guidance needed to help you untangle complex challenges and take effective, empowering action.

3. Elevate Your Practice Program *(6-Month Business Coaching)*
Ready to grow your practice sustainably while preserving your energy and values? **Elevate Your Practice** is a six-month coaching programme tailored for private practice dietitians who want to grow a thriving, profitable business without burning out. This will help you to:

- Build strong, sustainable business systems.
- Increase your income by charging confidently for your value.
- Attract and retain your ideal clients.
- Create a purposeful business lifestyle aligned with your values.

This isn't a generic business course. It's a trusted, proven pathway to build a values-aligned, confident, and thriving practice. With expert coaching and practical tools, Elevate Your Practice helps you grow both as a practitioner and a business owner, so you can achieve the impact, income, and independence you're aiming for.

Want to Take It Even Further?

You don't have to go it alone. At Elevated Dietetics, I'm here to support you, whether it's through a free download, a powerful one-on-one session, or six months of guided coaching.

These tools are designed to help you grow confidently, run your practice sustainably, and build a career that fits your life and values. Because when dietitians like you thrive, the people you support, and your profession benefit too.

Next Steps
- **Download** your free Business Plan Template
- **Book** a Get It Done session
- **Apply** for the next intake of the Elevate Your Practice Program

Visit www.elevateddietetics.com.au to access these offers and learn more.

I can't wait to support you in creating the private practice career you deserve.

*Coming Soon –
2026 release*

The Profitable Dietitian

Where purpose meets profit in private practice.

You've built your confidence.
Now it's time to build your income, impact,
and independence.

The Profitable Dietitian is the essential sequel to *The Confident Dietitian* — designed for dietitians who are ready to go beyond mindset and step into mastery of private practice business skills.

Join the waitlist or follow updates at
www.elevateddietetics.com.au

www.ingramcontent.com/pod-product-compliance
Lightning Source LLC
Chambersburg PA
CBHW042319090526
44584CB00030BA/4068